This Was OUR MALVERN

Volume 1

Compiled by
Margaret Bramford

MALCHIK MEDIA

A Malchik Media & richardlynttonbooks Publication

Published by

Malchik Media & richardlynttonbooks

Copyright © 2022 Richard C.G. Lyntton

ISBN: 979-8-9860794-3-1

Library of Congress Control Number: 2022909930

Cover and interior repackaging by Gary A. Rosenberg ~
www.thebookcouple.com

About the cover image:

Donkeys on Malvern Hills in the early 1900s

Thank you in advance for reading
This Was OUR Malvern ~
Worcestershire & Malvern
History Series Book 2

• • • • • • • • • • • • • • • • • •

You might also enjoy *From Cottage to Palace* ~
Worcestershire & Malvern History Series Book 1
https://www.amazon.com/dp/B09WB2LQHM
and the audiobook on Audible:
https://www.audible.com/pd/From-Cottage-
to-Palace-Audiobook/B0B3PQTSGZ
and
Upton-Upon-Severn Recollections ~
Worcestershire & Malvern History Series Book 3
https://www.amazon.com/gp/product/B0B1QX1BZ8

For more information about the Worcestershire
& Malvern History Series by Margaret Bramford,
or to sign up for our FREE richardlynttonbooks
(fiction and nonfiction) newsletter,
VISIT this richardlynttonbooks website link:
https://richardlynttonbooks.com/contact/

This Was OUR Malvern, Volume 1

A light-hearted social history of Malvern, Worcestershire, UK. These are the memories of one hundred and twenty-five Malvern and surrounding district people, recorded by the author. For the most part, they reflect Malvern life in the 1920's, 1930's and 1940's.

The author dedicates this book, with gratitude, to those Malvern people who readily shared their recollections—wise and valuable anecdotes and social history insights—with her. She has preserved their robust, individual, lively speech and their cheerful attitude to life.

Contents

• • • • • • • • • •

11 ~ We Went Shopping, 147

Mosaic of Malvern in 1972

Grey Gothic houses hang like flags
On flanks of homely, peaceful hills,
Clothed in a mediaeval garb of bracken brown,
Patterned with flashes of gold gorse
And shifting sheep.
History broods heavily, amid softened folds
Of ancient camps.
The flitting yellow-hammer's wistful song
Recalls the elegiac melodies
That Elgar plucked from melting Malvern air.

Magnolias magnanimous
Stand graciously in Priory Park
With memories of grandeur and of Shaw.
Mellow as a russet apple, glows the Priory,
Pink and purple in the flowering dusk.

Past tidy walls of mauve Malvern granite
On wet Sundays in winter
Jerk brown crocodiles of schoolgirls.
Schoolboys in a grey battalion
Chatter like yellow-capped sparrows.
Two walk alone, behind,
Eluding the patient master.

School bells punctuate your promenade
Past drowsy summer gardens,
Peopled with tall and ancient trees.

Winter evenings: owls hoot warily in the copse.
Summer evenings: woodpecker's merry laugh
Is heard above the traffic's whirr.
An excited crowd emerges from the pulsing theatre,
Chattering, flattering, scattering ...
Wistaria's heavy perfume drifts around.

A summer dawn ... a blackbird's woodwind notes
And pigeons' lulling melody ...
Along the sloping street a cheerful postman plods.
A strident school bell greets the Malvern day.

Margaret Bramford

1 ~ The Hills Are Alive!

"They never cease to amaze me, with their variable light and colour, and their changing moods." So said Geoffrey Boaz about his daily view of Malvern Hills, from his home at Rhydd Farm, Hanley Castle.

"The hills are our barometer", he declared. "They mirror the weather for the day. And sometimes they disappear completely from view!"

They *are* capricious. Do we admire them most on a calm, sunny day in February, with their subtle olive greens and browns? Or mysterious, in autumn, clad in a monkish Mediaeval cloak of russet bracken and burnished copper leaves? Or coldly blue and foreboding, in winter twilight, against a dramatic pink sky? Or dark, serene, and majestic, against a theatrical flaming summer sunset? Malvern and Malvern Hills are inseparable."

"I fell in love with them," confessed Marjorie Chater Hughes. "It was on a snowy day in January, during the war. When I arrived from London, at Colwall station, I looked up at the hills. They were snow-capped, just like a Japanese painting. I said, then and there, 'I want to live and die here!' And it looks as if I might!"

"Let's wave to Uncle Joe Stalin!" cried my teasing Uncle George, as the Bramford family climbed to the summit of British Camp, in the mid 1930's. And he was not wrong in his assumption that due East from the Malverns, the next highest

1

land is the Ural Mountains in Soviet Russia. The Worcester-shire Beacon is 425 metres high."

"I run a lot on the hills," said David Burley, in 1998. "I find them a wonderful, relaxing place. If you're feeling jaded, you come back in a totally different frame of mind. I go up on the hills, whatever the weather, when I'm training for the London Marathon. And I've done four of those!" (He ran his sixth in the year 2000.)

"We used the hills as a pleasant short cut, from West Malvern to Great Malvern, in the war," said a West Malvern resident. "We would climb steep Croft Bank, past St. James's School, up the zig-zag path and down through Happy Valley. We did this at all times of day. Malvern was a safe place then."

Apparently, West Malvern people walked this route in rain, fog, and snow, and back home from evening Art classes, in darkness. 'No torch was needed in the wartime blackout,' I was told. 'You *see* with your feet. The trees were our guide'.

Thus, barometric, aesthetic, therapeutic, or a walker's delight—the Malvern Hills nurture us, and sustain us, in different ways.

Geologists tell us that our hills are 670 million years old. In parts, they could well be 1,000 million years old—which reduces us humans to microscopic specks.

Malvern stone is like solidified lava, formed under heat and pressure. Its colours are extremely variable: dark green and black from hornblende, pink from feldspar, purple blue from dolerite.

I like Catherine Moody's description of Malvern stone, in her book, "The Silhouette of Malvern". "Next to its hardness and endurance, its chief peculiarity is the irregular cleavage. When it splits, its shape is entirely without symmetry. Its variable colours are mingled together in a pepper and salt mixture. Different Malvern quarries used to yield their own special colours.

Dark and often gloomy in appearance, Malvern walls can present a very rich façade. Malvern stone's crooked shapes, its planes askew, and its ridged bumpy surface produce a singular unquiet and restlessness."

Jack Lewis told me: "The stone masons of Malvern described the awkward shapes of Malvern stone as 'like 'osses' 'eads'. To build them into a wall was like constructing a jigsaw puzzle. Generous mortar is needed."

It is an old custom to crown the garden walls in Malvern with irregular blocks of Malvern stone. I look out for the line-up of 'osses' 'eads', peering over the wall wherever I walk. Sling Lane has good examples.

"Naturalists appreciate the Malvern Hills for the rare High Brown Fritillary butterfly," says Dudley Brook. "The Malvern Hills are like a little island, with a variety of habitats, from boggy to moorland. Adders are becoming scarce, so we Conservators preserve the bracken cover they need."

David Whitehorne of Malvern Hills Conservators spoke to me: "Familiar sights on the hills are soaring Buzzards, diving and singing Skylarks, and Stonechats amongst the gorse bushes.

Rare birds of passage feed on the hills—Snow Bunting and Ring Ouzel. Rare mammals make their home on Malvern Hills—the Lesser Horseshoe Bat, the Dormouse, and the Polecat."

Edwin Lees, the Worcestershire naturalist, was staying at South Cottage, above Malvern Wells, in the summer of 1841, when he awoke to a well-known phenomenon.

"A little before 5 a.m. I was surprised to perceive that the prospect was **all sea.** Bredon Hill in the distance, peered its head out of the waters, like an islet afloat on the waves ... All the clouds had apparently crept quietly below during the night, and now lay calm as the stillest lake. All above was pure and blue, as a laughing infant's eyes.

At length, about seven o'clock, the cloudy ocean gave signs of life, rolled in dense columns to the base of the hills, scaled rock after rock and smoked away finally into mid-air. A **melting** day followed."

But the hills are a sociable venue too. Their spine tingles with the tramp of walkers' feet, especially at weekends and Bank Holidays. It is then that the hills become populated like a small town, when people of all ages admire the exhilarating views on **both** sides of the hills' backbone.

Frank Bowers recalls: "As children, on Bank Holidays, Mother would pack us up sandwiches. We would start at the North Hill and walk all along the hills and back again—an 18-mile walk."

Mary Davis echoes this. "Our good neighbour was a children's nurse. On a Sunday, she would take us from Colwall to the British Camp or Eastnor Monument, and for a picnic there in summer. All I've learned about nature and birds, I've learned from her."

Freda Morris remembers: "I had to look after my two sisters, who were 2½ and 1 years old. I would take them for walks on the hills from St. Ann's Well. We would take a picnic and walk for miles. We wore out our clothes sliding down!"

Mary Wells also slid down the hills—on a piece of cardboard. "You could virtually slide from the top of the Beacon down to St. Ann's Well, non-stop," she boasted.

Doris Smith, aged 97, told me: "Donkeys would take us children on to the Horseshoe Walk, or up Happy Valley, or to Ivy Scar Rock. We would picnic at Dripping Well and take a methylated stove and a kettle, for tea. When it snowed, we had toboggans. There was a special toboggan track above Happy Valley."

Jim Tudge remembers The Pink Cottage Tea Garden on the hills, "where we had boiled eggs and lovely brown bread."

Joan Preece said, "As children we walked from Poolbrook along the Wells Road to Little Malvern, and under the hills to the Pink Cottage. Mrs. Baldwin lived there. She gave us boiled eggs to eat. We had them at home too, but they tasted *special* in the Pink Cottage."

In a broadcast on the BBC in 1944, the legendary Alice Betteridge said, "I'm the fourth generation to keep sheep on Malvern hills, and the third generation to run donkeys. Whole families from Birmingham would come to our donkey stands in the morning, with their picnic baskets. Tiny children would travel in panniers at the side of the saddle. They loved it! There was always a donkey show in Crown Meadow. Mother and granny took prizes every year."

"My brother was a donkey boy," said Ellen Hymas. "He worked for Mrs. Betteridge. She lived on North Hill and kept a dozen donkeys near the Unicorn Inn. They went up Red Lion Bank to Happy Valley. My brother would be paid sixpence to take the donkey and its rider to the Toposcope. He was allowed to ride back. He earned one and sixpence a week."

"My treat was a sixpenny ride on a donkey called Lady. That was **my** donkey," said Joy Van Daesdonk.

A Malvern Wells painter of Malvern Hills donkeys was Mary Brandling (1823-1873). There is quite a Spanish,

Andalucian atmosphere in her paintings. Against pale brown rocks, stand patient donkeys with panniers. Seated on the ground, beside baskets of produce, are local country women, in their long black skirts, red shawls and frilled bonnets. The donkeys and the red shawls evoke Spanish Sierras—yet we know full well that these people and animals are overlooking the Severn plain!

The hills can offer refuge too. Mary Tudge worked at West Malvern school for 25 years. She told me: "We had one child who kept running away in school time. He used to go up on the hills. We had to go and look for him or get his parents. I've met him recently, now grown-up. He confessed, 'Yes, I used to be hiding in the bushes and listening for my grand-father looking for me'."

The Malvern Hills Conservators have preserved our hills for over one hundred years. "They are the best hills in the world," enthused Geoffrey Chiswell, "but a little bit overgrown. Too many sycamores. They obscure the view, compared with the views painted by A.R. Quinton in the 1920's."

Naturally, the hills are a place of inspiration for painters, writers, and musicians. Our Worcestershire composer, Sir Edward Elgar, often walked on them. They are also a place for meditation. On 22nd February 1999, Thinking Day was celebrated by local Girl Guides on Malvern Hills.

And as a final resting place? Midge Tompkins spoke: "I love Malvern Hills. I used to walk for miles over the hills with our dog. The ashes of my daughter and of my husband, John Tompkins, are in a garden, right up on the hills. I've just ordered a rose to go there, called 'Remember Me'."

And to celebrate special anniversaries? Derek Davidson reminded me: "Beacons were lit on Worcestershire Beacon to commemorate Queen Elizabeth II's accession to the throne in 1952, and again in 1995 for the 50th Anniversary of VE Day."

I remember seeing Beacons on the hills in 1988 to commemorate England's victory over the Spanish Armada in 1588. More recently, we saw the Millennium Beacon on Malvern Hills.

Elsie Godsell of Colwall commented appropriately, "When my mother lived at the Wyche cutting as a girl, she told us what wonderful sunrises they had over the Severn plain. But we here, on the ***other*** side of the hills have the wonderful ***sunsets!***"

We will let an anonymous schoolgirl of St. James's School. West Malvern, have the last word about Malvern Hills, in the early 1930's:

"We visited the Pink Cottage on the hills. They gave us tea there and we were allowed to roam the hills. ***It was there that I first felt their power and beauty.***"

2 ~ Malvern Water

∙ ∙ ∙ ∙ ∙ ∙ ∙ ∙ ∙ ∙ ∙ ∙ ∙ ∙ ∙ ∙ ∙ ∙ ∙ ∙

Our Queen, when she travels abroad,
Must never be ill, or look bored.
MALVERN WATER she takes,
(A fine 'cuppa' it makes),
Drinks it 'neat', and her health is assured.

(From a Malvern Women's Institute
Limerick Competition)

"It's wonderful stuff!" exclaimed David Burley. "I drink a lot of it. When we go on holiday, we always take big containers of Malvern water with us. We follow the example of the Queen!"

"I buy Malvern water by the case," said 80-year-old Vivien Bowkley. "I used to collect it at the waterspout. It's foolish not to drink it, when you live here.

We once visited one of the places where Schweppes obtain their water," she continued. "Just beyond British Camp, as you go down the hill to Colwall. Inside, it's like an enormous swimming pool, white tiled. The water, in depth, looks a beautiful aquamarine. It's extraordinary!

And it's piped down to Colwall and bottled there. Our guide said they do nothing to it. 'We simply filter it—and there's never anything in the filter. It's quite pure.' Then we went round Schweppes factory."

Schweppes, who bottle Malvern water, have been associated with Malvern since 1851. They use a spring which has been in regular use since 250 B.C. and provides water of matchless and consistent purity.

For a million years, water has been welling up in Springs in the Malvern Hills—since the retreat of the Ice Age glaciers. Where Malvern water originates is a mystery. Some say it comes underground, under the sea, from Sweden. Others say the Alps.

"Malvern water has **made** Malvern," commented George Sayer. "To get Victorian people to walk over the hills, and drink water at various springs was very beneficial for them. Especially if they had spent much of their lives over-eating and over-drinking. People on the continent revere their spas more than we do."

Gary Taylor said, "I was a pupil for some time at the Open Air School, West Malvern. We used to call in at St. Ann's Well and drink from the fountain. The water was nice and cool, especially on a hot day!"

"It's good for people's rheumatism," added Doris Smith. "That well water tastes **sweet**".

"Cuffs used to bottle the water at Holy Well," said Mary Davis, "and make ginger beer and lemonade. I did their typing and bookkeeping."

"I had a lot of trouble with styes on my eyes, as a child," said Joy Van Daesdonk. "When we lived at Malvern Wells, I would visit the Eye Well, a small trickle behind Holy Well. It was always very cold and clean. It was comforting, as there were no antibiotics then."

Joy had further memories of Malvern water. "There was a Tea Room at Malvern Wells. They made the tea from spring water. It does make an awfully big difference to the *flavour* of the tea!"

Joy recalled, nostalgically, the old-style Pump Room at the Winter Gardens in the early 1930's. "I liked the Pump Room. The little cherubs fountain flowed generously in those days, and you could drink from its glasses. There were lots of potted palms. The Lloyd Loom tables and chairs were a pinky colour and had sheets of glass on the tabletops.

In the cafe at the side, all the teapots and water jugs were silver coloured. You could get a proper afternoon tea. I can still taste their strawberry ice cream!"

Marjorie Chater Hughes is a sprightly 92-year-old (1998), who drinks water from a deep, deep well in Malvern. "A lovely woman brings me four of those huge bottles of well water every week, so I don't have to go up to the hills!"

Mary Wells had a gruesome story to tell about water. "At our bungalow in Madresfield Road, we were still using oil lamps up to 1956, and well water. In 1949, we had a drought. My father took the top off the well and there were ten dead rats floating on the water. And we had been drinking that water for many years! So, he took a sample to Manders the chemist, to get it analysed. He did not tell them what he had discovered. They said, 'That's perfectly fine, Mr. Wood. Go on drinking it.' It makes you wonder how fussy we are these days. God knows how long those rats had been there!"

"The Spa water of Tenbury Wells was not good for every-one," said Frances Milsom, who lived there as a child. "I had a goitre, a throat swelling, from that water. It gave you 'Derbyshire necks'. The doctor prescribed water for me from chemists in Birmingham.

Every day, that water came to Tenbury Wells for me in a big

stone jar. My father fetched it from the railway station. Then I went to stay with my uncle in Wales, and suddenly the goitre started to disappear to the relief of our doctor."

"Personally, I drink the water from Earl Beauchamp's spout in Cowleigh Road," said Roland Bannister. "We fill up there once a week."

At 105-years-old (in 1999), and blind, Elizabeth Guise Berrow, born and bred in Malvern, is nevertheless very alert and up to date. A fellow resident in her Rest Home told me, "Elizabeth knows all the answers to our crossword puzzles! When asked by a journalist what was her secret for a long life, Elizabeth replied, "A glass of cold Malvern water". This sounds like an excellent advertisement.

3 ~ In Praise of Malvern

"I was born and bred in Malvern, and I'm glad I've never left it," said Arthur Russell of Malvern Link to me, in his 90th year. "The furthest I've been out of England was to [the island of] Jersey."

George 'Divvy' Davis, the well-known local beekeeper, echoed this sentiment: "I was away at war for three years. And I've never been away since! There's so much to do here—my house in Lower Wyche and doing my bees and that. And there's plenty of scope for going out anywhere. It's all here! Why go abroad?"

"Malvern is a beautiful place—the hills, the flowers, the houses," declared Maria Lloyd Foulkes in her 91st year. "During the war and before, Malvern was a very simple place, a very happy place. I am very happy to be here still. Life is never dull here."

Her daughter, Ornella, commented: "In the 1930's, between the wars, Malvern had *style*."

"I like living in Malvern, where I was born," said Joan Preece. "I wouldn't want to leave it. And I like it in Hayes Bank, on the common, 'cos we've got such a lovely view of the hills."

Elsie Jennings was indebted to Malvern air and Malvern water for a different reason: "My father worked for a baker in Bath, and that's where he met my mother. He delivered bread to the house where she was in service. They married in Bath.

But my mother was a Malvern-born girl. She kept writing to *her* mother who was in Malvern. And after my mother's six-year marriage there was no sign of children. So, *her* mother said, 'If you come back to Malvern, you *will* have children.' My parents took her advice and came to live in Malvern. And within twelve months my mother had two children! That was me and my sister!"

Gary Taylor told me: "I loved my time, as a boy, at the Open Air School, West Malvern. In fact, coming from the Black Country, I fell in love with the place the second I saw it. I said to my father, 'Dad, I'm going to live in Malvern when I grow up.' And I did! I've been working at Malvern Link station now for the past twenty-five years. I've enjoyed it very much."

Victorian ladies were equally impressed by the beauty of Malvern and its surrounding villages. Anna Boobbyer wrote: "In May 1855, our dear mother took us to lovely Malvern, for five months. We came from London, by train to Worcester. We drove to Malvern on the top of a four-horse stagecoach. The apple and cherry orchards were in rich bloom and perfection. We spent a happy summer in Malvern."

Mary Munslow Jones, as a little girl, had a very special recollection of Malvern. It was in early June of 1925, during a spell of fine weather. "I had been with my parents, from Dorset, where we lived, to visit elderly relatives in the Midlands. I was very glad to be returning home. In those days, children had to endure absolute tedium, sitting on prickly horsehair sofas, in a stuffy house in a stuffy town. Not even a book to read! As the train ran home southwards, towards Bristol, I looked through the carriage window, and saw a range of hills of distinctive outline. 'Those are the Malvern Hills,' said my father. In the meadow below the train, haymaking was in full swing, with wagons and shire horses. Women in sunbonnets, tending the hay, leaned on their wooden hay rakes, and waved to the train. How I envied the children playing there among the haycocks! The vision of that happy little scene, with the blue line of the hills in the background, has remained with me ever since."

Mary Munslow Jones, in adult life, was destined to live in the Malvern area. As a keen member of the Worcestershire Naturalists, she got to know and love the Malvern Hills intimately.

4 ~ Characters

A Comforting Thought for the Senior Citizen:
Some people, the older they are,
Grow faces, say, somewhat bizarre.
But my face I don't mind it,
For I am behind it.
The person in front gets the jar!

(From a Malvern Women's Institute
Limerick Competition)

Malvern has grown from a cluster of villages around the base of the Malvern Hills. And small communities generate interesting and eccentric individuals long remembered even after they have left the scene.

POLLY CARTLAND

She was the mother of the famous Dame Barbara Cartland, the romantic novelist, and lived in Poolbrook at Littlewood House.

"She was lovely," said Francis Bird. "She was a great friend of my mother's. She would ask, 'Is there anything I can do for you, Mrs. Bird? Can I bring you anything from the shop?'

"Off went Polly in her little black Austin 35. She would back out of her driveway and pull into the middle of the road and stop there. Not much traffic then. Then she would get out and go and shut the gates, 'cos of the dogs. She would go up Langridge Road, and you could still hear her in the same first gear 'till she got to the Golf House at the top. She would stay in her car and expect shopkeepers to come out to her for her order.

Before the Second World War, she had a swimming pool built in her garden. Her two sons invited the Youth Clubs of Poolbrook and Barnards Green to swim there, free of charge. Polly Cartland would come down to the swimming pool in her long black skirt, with her two little Scottie dogs, one black, one white. She was only about five feet tall, and she always put her hands on her hips.

Sadly, her two sons were killed within a few days of each other in the war. From that time, the swimming pool was drained, and it was never used again. She would have nothing done to it, 'cos it had been made 'for my boys'.

There was a nice side to her. As choirboys, we had to sing carols every Christmas Eve in her front room. It was a beautiful purple velvet-clad room. Ken Wiggins, the Choirmaster, and Miss Robinson, the organist, used to start us off. Polly always gave us two mince pies each and a threepenny piece. But we never had the threepence 'cos that had to go into church funds!"

Doris Smith told me: "Polly Cartland was a member of Malvern Women's Institute. She gave us a lovely talk on "My 85 years of life". Someone from the Art College had done sketches of the dresses worn every ten years of her life. She had such a raucous voice that we used to say, 'She's like a corncrake with asthma!'

For our August meeting, she invited us all to her house in Poolbrook. She had prepared all sorts of Treasure Hunts in the garden. But it was wet. She provided us with tea, and we had indoor games for two hours. She was able to find seating for 21 of us. It was a most entertaining time. As we left, there was a thunderstorm."

Joan Preece of Poolbrook remembered Polly too, for her hospitality. "She was Chairman of first Malvern Scouts, and I was on the committee. Polly would invite the committee and some parents to a dinner in her home. She hired waiters from local hotels. It was a grand affair. There would be a big log fire in the huge chimney grate—almost too hot for comfort!

Upstairs in her bedroom, where we left our coats, everything was *pink*—all the furniture, carpets, and curtains. And I have noticed that pink was *still* her famous daughter, Barbara's, favourite colour for her dresses!"

BARBARA CARTLAND

Francis Bird recalled: "When Barbara Cartland used to come, as a young lady, to stay with her mother in Poolbrook, before the war, and her brothers were there too, you could hear *her* at the bottom of the village. She could *talk* ... She shouted!"

Hilda Shinn had a special memory of Barbara Cartland when both were young girls. "My family lived in Guarlford Road, in a very old black and white house, which is 500 years old. We were beekeepers and had 70 hives. We used to show our honey all over the country and we won a lot of cups.

Barbara Cartland was very fond of honey. She used to come and buy 14-pound tins from us. She used it for everything— even for face cream and rubbed it all over her skin. Now she's nearly 100 and she's not grown old. We spent many happy times talking in our garden. She was a wonderful person."

N.B. Barbara Cartland has become "The best selling author in the world" according to the Guinness Book of World Records. She has written an average of 23 romantic novels a year.

"NAVVY LIZ"

Ivy Pitt of West Malvern told me about this colourful lady, Elizabeth Webb. "She lived where the West Malvern Post Office is now. She wore a long skirt, two or three cardigans, brogue shoes and a man's top hat with little feathers round the band. She would climb on the roof to replace a tile. In her cottage were metal trunks, full of old watches. At the top of the stairs was the biggest aspidistra ever seen! And she had some donkeys."

Marjorie King remembered: "Miss Webb had the Post Office. She always wore a top hat. She used to ride around the village in a carriage pulled by a horse. She had a sweet [candy] shop. We all used to go to Sunday School and spend half our collection on sweets [candy] there!"

"WALKING JOHN"

Frank Bowers recalled: "There was a man who lived in Ranelagh Road, Malvern Link. His name was Preece. He was a tailor who worked for Pembridge's, the Outfitters in the Link [Malvern Link]. He loved walking. As a boy, I remember I was with Father, and Father knew him and asked him, "Have you been far today, John?" Walking John replied, "Oh, I've been out to Pershore this morning and back. But the dog's tired. So, I've left him at home. I'm going for a walk on my own."

He wore a mauve velvet coat with a fitted cape. Years after when Mr. Pembridge retired from the shop, he lived in the alms houses at Newland. John Preece used to collect Mr. Pembridge's newspapers in the Link, take them down to Newland and get them there by 7 o'clock every morning. "Walking John" would regularly walk to Upton, Ledbury or even to Hereford and back."

MISS CALEY

Several people remembered her vividly. Francis Bird said, "She lived in the big house on the corner of Tibberton and Imperial Roads. She used to keep her horse in the back kitchen. The hay for the horse was in the front room. Miss Caley wore a long black dress and a big black shawl and a black felt hat. You could hardly see her in her trap 'cos she used to crouch down.

She had lights on her trap. She would go to sleep in the trap at night and the horse would bring her home. She used to take logs of wood to an old friend out in Welland at night. It would be pitch black and she would still be trundling home fast asleep. People used to ring up the police and say, 'Miss Caley's just gone past and she's asleep'. 'Yes, we know', they replied, 'cos she always told the police where she was going.

Miss Caley had her mother living with her. The day her mother died; her mother was reading the newspaper in the front bedroom. Where the paper was open then, it was still open at the same page when Miss Caley herself died. She had left the bedroom exactly as it was.

She used to go to the Priory [cathedral] every Sunday and leave a nice offertory for them. Of course, she was Caley's Chocolates. She was rather a wealthy woman."

Dennis Morgan, the blacksmith at Barnards Green recalled Miss Caley. "We used to shoe her horse, Tommy. She was strange. Up came her sash window and out came the horse droppings. She would ride about in the night in this pony and trap, with hurricane lamps dangling. She used to collect wood and take it to poor people. There she was, huddled up in this trap, on a cold winter's night. It was an eerie sight!"

Heather Talbot told me: "Miss Caley would come on dark winter evenings to visit a grave in Malvern Wells cemetery. Huddled in coats and scarves, she perched on top of the driving seat, and seemed unaware of those she passed. We girls would be going home from Girl Guides. We would rush past her because in the mist, it was quite a ghostly sight!"

George Morris had even more interesting details to tell me: "Miss Caley was a great member of the Priory Church, so she knew my father, who was Custos there. She drove all over Malvern in a horse and trap. She was short and dressed in black. To most of us she looked like a witch. But in conversation, she was a very well-read lady, bright and very interesting to talk to. She used to sell eggs. She went out to Castlemorton, bought these eggs, and sold them again. We always got our eggs from her. But she wasn't short of money.

Her sister was Mrs. Damsel, who used to ride a bicycle—an equally strange lady, but she wore gay colours in contrast to Miss Caley. Mrs. Damsel had married her tutor. *He* was known as 'the blessed', alluding to Christina Rossetti's poem, THE BLESSED DAMOZEL.

They were very generous people. Mrs. Damsel always gave mince pies to a fête. But they would have to be hidden, 'cos nobody could eat them. They were baked so hard!"

"BLIND GEORGE"

"You could whistle a tune to him, and he would play it on his harmonium at once", recalled Arthur Russell.

Generations of visitors to St. Ann's Well heard "Blind George" Pullen playing on his harmonium or dulcitone every day for over 50 years. He began playing there in the 1880's, walking the four miles over the hills from Storridge, where he lived. Later, he lived at Lower Wyche.

Joan Preece often saw him, when she was a child: "He used to often play the Edwardian waltz 'White Wings, they never grow weary'."

"As children," related Albert Layland, "when we met him on the hills, we used to ask him the time. He told us by feeling the hands of his fob watch."

Disney Reynolds remembered "Blind George" when he played for dances at Trinity Church Hall. "He used to arrive at 8 o'clock and play till 2 in the morning. And he could *play* that piano—especially if he'd had some beer! We had some marvellous times there."

Dorothy Pembridge said: "My uncle would fetch "Blind George" in a horse-drawn cab to play for dances in the Playroom at Madresfield Court. They primed him with beer, and as the evening wore on, he was playing hymn tunes in waltz time!"

CALEB FOXWELL

He had a tailor's shop next to the White Horse pub in Great Malvern. His tailors sat down, legs crossed, to make suits.

MISS JENKINS

"She lived in Victoria Road and was a very strange lady," said Frank Bowers. "When she travelled by train, she reserved a compartment. The Station Master of Malvern Link had to meet her and conduct her to her carriage and lock the door. No one could get near to speak to her. She wore "cartwheel" hats and always wore a thick veil over her face, which was covered with white powder. She was comfortably off but when she died, they found about forty cats living in her house. It was in a terrible state."

"When I worked in the restaurant on The Promenade, Great Malvern," said Elsie Jennings, "Miss Jenkins came regularly for supper there. Old Mr. Griffith would bring her in a horse-drawn cab. She wore huge hats and elegant lace collars and cuffs.

One day, I had to go down with a colleague to her house to get the money she owed. Oh, the house was full of cats! The cats' saucers were all over the kitchen!"

MISS SANTLER

"She was a sister to the Santler brothers who made the first motor car," said Dorothy Jones. "She lived next door to us. She used to see me hanging on to my twin sisters, bringing them home from school. Miss Santler wore long skirts and rode a 'sit-up-and-beg' bicycle. She once showed us her old "Britannia" costume made out of maps of the British Empire."

WALLY WESTON

"He kept the Foresters Arms", at Barnards Green, said Francis Bird. "He had a cork leg. He had lost his leg in the Navy in the first world war. He trained boxers.

When we were on our way to school, we would see him running like a stag with these boxers. With his walking stick, he would hop and run, hop, and run with the boxers, all the way down Guarlford Road.

One of his major boxers was Jack Hood, who was the British champion. They also went to a gym at Madresfield Court. Wally wore a cowboy hat—a Stetson."

"Wally Weston was a great friend of my father's," said Mary Wells. "Tommy Farr, a famous boxer, came to Malvern to be trained by Wally Weston. Wally was masseur to Richard Lygon of Madresfield Court. Wally entertained the Lygon family in the back room of the Foresters Arms, which he owned. I've sat on their laps! When I was about 12, Wally would say to me, 'Go in and meet the Lygons'. And Lady Sibell and Lady Mary would be there."

HARRY BURLEY

His grandson, David Burley described him. "My grandfather joined the Priory choir in 1920. He stayed in the choir for 50 years. He was also a comedian singer as well, at local concerts. In the 1930's he was very well known for his comedy songs— Edwardian Music Hall songs like Phil the fluter's Ball. Lots of old ladies remember that he wore a comical little hat on elastic on the side of his head. They would be in hoots of laughter, seeing his hat bobbing up and down."

Jim Tudge said, "When I was about 17 years old, Harry Burley, my hairdresser, had just discovered my first grey hairs. He was always trying to sell me hair restorer that he made himself. But he himself was as bald as a coot! It seems to run in the family. Harry Burley was a great character, reciting those old-fashioned poems."

BILLY GAMMON

This handsome and popular Dance Band leader with his All-Star Players attracted audiences from all over the Midlands to Malvern. Win Foster was a keen dancer. She said, "Billy Gammon's band in the 1930's would play on the Winter Gardens terrace or on the Priory Park bandstand every day—morning and afternoon—and on Saturday and Sunday evenings. His concerts of popular music were well attended, by people sitting on the grass in the park, in summer months."

Gordon Acock saw a different aspect of him. "Billy Gammon was a good engineer. In the war, he was only too keen to come and work at our place on turning and lathe work, so that he could stay home in Malvern in a reserved occupation—to keep the home fires burning and to raise our spirits by his band music."

THE BALLARD FAMILY OF COLWALL

"They were great pioneers of Colwall," said Elsie Godsell. "They built houses and planted trees. They had a canning factory. They had orchards. They canned all their fruit—pears, plums, damsons, cherries. During the war I could buy their canned fruit on points, to sell in my little shop in Colwall. It was very useful."

BAGNALL O'REILLY

He was a character recalled by Dorothy Jones. "He wore a bowler hat and was dressed in black. He would talk to you over the fence. Mum was planting some flowers in the garden, in the front. He said to Mum, "That's the right plant you want in your garden. Marigolds. You want to marry gold. A good motto!"

CLEM WALTON

"I am the daughter of Clem Walton, the photographer," said Joan Preece. "My father was also a hairdresser and barber. He had his own little wooden shop in Court Road.

He had a big bicycle with a great big square carrier on the front. He used old-fashioned cameras. He would put a black velvet cover over his head, and he looked through it to photograph his clients. He would go miles on that bicycle, taking wedding photos. People from all over the area say to me, 'Oh, your father took my wedding photo!' One of his main jobs was to take photos of the Girls' College pupils every year.

They were glass plates in those days. He would dry the photos outside the shop and be up half the night developing them in the little darkroom. He would have all these negatives retouched by a lady named Mrs. Walford. She lived in Frederick Road in Malvern Link.

I had a penny off my father to walk from Barnards Green all across the cricket fields to take these negatives to Mrs. Walford.

She did them while I waited. She took out all the wrinkles from people's faces and pencilled any blemishes over. Then it was very smart.

My father took a lot of photos for the *Malvern Gazette*. And he went to people's houses to take photos. He worked for Sir Edmund Lechmere at Severn End. My father took photos of Sir Edmund, with all the trophies he had shot when abroad— the heads of big game, shot in Africa. Those photos were on show for a long time in his shop. He took all his equipment on his bicycle. I used to go with him sometimes."

TROYTE GRIFFITH

"He taught me perspective", said the artist, Catherine Moody. "My father, Victor Hume Moody's drawing of Troyte, captures the restless, energetic characteristics of this well-known Malvern architect." Elgar depicts the same boundless energy of Troyte, his friend, in the seventh of his Enigma Variations.

"He was known as 'The Giddy Ninepin', continued Catherine Moody, "because Troyte Griffith wore a faded green tweed jacket and knickerbocker trousers, a tweed cap, and was tall and thin with a round head. In winter, he wore an old cape of the same faded green, which he had brought from Austria. His spectacles were steel-rimmed. His bicycle was tall too. His attractive watercolours reveal his love of Malvern.

Troyte had noticeably long teeth. He was known as 'Tusker', at Harrow, where his father was Science master. On one occasion in Malvern, I heard George Bernard Shaw ask, 'Has Troyte Griffith still got those awful teeth?'"

In the late '20's and early '30's, Jim Tudge would often see Troyte Griffith and Elgar walking or cycling together in Malvern. Troyte would make a daily visit to the Bluebird Tea Rooms often with Sir Edward Elgar.

"When I went to W. James, the builders, to work," said Jim Tudge, "I heard that we were Troyte Griffith's favourite builders, so I would meet him. His drawings were absolutely wonderful. He was most meticulous in everything and would come to inspect the joinery as it was being made—quite unlike modern architects! All his specifications were written in his lovely handwriting.

One day, he said to me he would like to see some catalogues of windows. Metal windows had just come in then. So, I brought him a Crittall catalogue. There was a picture of a lady looking out of a window. Troyte turned to me and said, 'It's *windows* I want,—not women!' He was supposed to be a misogynist."

CANON DEANE

He was a school chaplain and everything else at St. James's School, West Malvern. A former pupil describes him: "He was multi-talented. He used to skip about, coaching the tennis six in summer; blow his whistle furiously on the hockey field in winter; write a weekly contribution for Punch. He was an inspiring teacher; preached witty and sensible sermons and prepared us in his own kind way for confirmation."

MISS SEVERN BURROW

She was a County Councillor. She planned the Open Air School in West Malvern in the 1920's. It was for children from the Birmingham area who needed fresh air and good food.

MR. QUARTERMAIN

Ivy Pitt told me: "Mr. Quartermain was a taxidermist, in West Malvern. So, we used to say, 'Mind your cats!' They said he sent the skins for gloves.

IVY FIELD

Elsie Godsell said: "She went to school with my sister Mary. Ivy lived at Evendine. She went to Madresfield Court as Lady's Maid. Later on, she became Dresser to the present Queen Mother. My sister and I were invited to Clarence House, home of the Queen Mother when Ivy was there.

I enjoyed Clarence House very much—meeting the famous corgi dogs and hearing Ivy's account of her latest Royal Tour abroad with the Queen Mother. We had tea there in Ivy's nice flat. She was a lovely person. After she retired, she lived in Worthing, near Brighton. Finally, she came back to Worcestershire, to the Beauchamp Community at Newland, near Malvern."

LADY EMILY FOLEY

Nancy Clay told me: "I was born in 1910 in Stoke Edith, Herefordshire. My father remembered Lady Foley there—she who owned the Manor of Malvern, but who lived in Stoke Edith. My father worked as a forester in the woods, and he was also employed in the gardens of Lady Foley's house. She was very generous, he said. She had several schools and churches built in Malvern.

She had Stoke Edith railway station built. They used to stop the express trains at Stoke Edith for her if she needed to go to Hereford. But she came to Great Malvern station by horse and carriage, to avoid the tunnels through the hills, if she wanted to catch a train to London. She had a special waiting room there, with her own furnishings."

THE MISS FITTONS

"There were five Miss Fittons", explained Disney Reynolds. "Miss Clare was the eldest and we were in her Bible class for years at Holy Trinity church. You had to learn the Collect every Sunday and recite it out loud.

Miss Hilda Fitton married a clerical man at a grand wedding at Trinity Church in 1911. Another sister, Monica, married Mr. Trew, Music Master. Isabel was the one portrayed by Elgar in the sixth of his Enigma Variations. They were a very musical family, and played, along with Elgar, in small orchestras, locally.

Holy Trinity church wanted some new gates for the north entrance. Miss Clare Fitton said to me, 'We're going to buy those gates, Disney.' I said, 'Why are *you* goin' to buy them?' And she replied, 'Three or four of us have used them more than anyone else. So, we're going to replace them.'"

THE MISS GOSDENS

"I knew them well," said Meriel Hodgetts. "There were two sets of twins—Daisy and Minnie, then Nina and Olive. They lived at The Cockshoot, Castlemorton Common, in a Georgian cottage, built about 1721, where they kept a lot of animals.

They were a lovely family! My mother and I did enjoy visiting them for tea, in our pony and trap. They had a terrific sense of humour. There was an enormous organ at their home, The Cock*shot*, as they pronounced it. The name came from the practice of driving woodcocks into a net, to catch them.

The Gosden sisters were all very musical. They taught music at schools in and around Malvern. And they all played in quartets and ensembles with Elgar, whom they knew well.

All four ladies played the organ at various churches. Minnie was organist at Birtsmorton Church, Daisy at West Malvern Church. Nina played the organ at Little Malvern Priory, where she had to ascend steep steps to the organ loft, and Olive was at Welland Church.

Nina played the double bass and was in great demand at Three Choirs Festivals. She would take her double bass with her in her little car, all wrapped up in a blanket. People would say that it looked like an old man, sitting there!

The Gosden sisters were real country folk, tall and neatly dressed, but not fashionable. They wore their hair with fringes. Before they acquired a car each, they would travel by horse and trap."

HOP MIDDLETON

Frances Milsom spent her childhood in Tenbury Wells. She recalled: "Hop Middleton was a funny old man. Every so often he would run out into the middle of the street and fire a gun! He had been in the army. All the children used to scatter but nobody got hurt. Even so, they were all frightened of him."

GRANNY ANDREWS AND GRANNY PRICE

"Granny Andrews had a little wooden sweetshop, cum cigarettes, cum drinks—" recalled Francis Bird, "—in Poolbrook. It was an ice cream parlour too and had the newspaper round. I delivered 13 papers I got from the Malvern Wells station, before arriving in her shop. And 29 more papers after that. She gave me 2 shillings and 3 pence a week.

Granny Andrews had a tea shop too. The Midland Red buses stopped outside her shop and the drivers would slip inside to have a cup of tea, with ha'penny buns. But she didn't make ice cream herself.

Granny Price ran an ice cream parlour next door to the dairy. The Ice Man came to Granny Price. He went to the fish shops too, with his big square blocks of ice. We had to push Granny Price's truck, containing the ice cream, up to Granny Andrew's shop 300 yards away. She would give us a ha'penny cornet of ice cream for doing that!"

John Hunt of Barnards Green remembered Granny Price. "She was a wonderful old lady. She went round the streets selling her homemade ice cream. She had a hand cart and a bell. All she had as transport looked a bit like a bedstead on two wheels."

MR. JOHN STALLARD

Elsie Godsell remembered two interesting gentlemen who lived in Colwall. "Mr. John Stallard, of The Redlands, was very fond of his garden. He grew peaches, pears and all the beautiful fruits. He would go to his office in Worcester by train from Colwall. Every morning, he wore a lovely flower in his buttonhole. Every Sunday, he enjoyed apple pie, which his cook always made for him. She had to preserve the apples in the autumn, so he could eat them all the year round."

THE REVEREND HARRIS

"He was a composer of music. He would go through the village of Colwall on his bicycle and, like Elgar, he was composing in his head as he went along. So absorbed was he, that he would come away from the fish shop with the fishmonger's bicycle instead of his own!"

5 ~ James Carty . . . The Perfect Gentleman

● ●

Before 1908, Malvern folk had never seen a black man, except in picture books, or when entertainers blacked their faces to become "Nigger Minstrels" as was then the acceptable title.

James Carty, from the West Indies, brought to Malvern in 1908, the exotic flavour of his island, Barbados. He brought spice to the work-a-day life of Barnards Green, romance to an English girl, and he established a dynasty of Cartys in Malvern.

His daughter, Alma Longstaff of Barnards Green, related to me the saga of James Carty's life. "He came to England in 1908. He was in the Merchant Navy. They used to leave the ship to work in different countries for three months—on fairs and circuses or fruit picking. Then they would return to their ship and sail for home.

Father joined Lord John Sanger's circus in 1908. My mother, Eliza Dance, and a friend, went to this circus when it was in Malvern. James Carty's work was to erect tents and unload the ropes and flooring for the Ring. After the show, he showed off the animals to the public. That's when he met my mother when she was looking at the animals. They got talking and arranged to meet again. The circus moved on to Worcester.

But James *walked* back from Worcester to meet my Mum.

They met each day for another week. He returned home to Barbados and got friends to write to her as he couldn't write well. Two years later, he came back to Malvern. He was 27. She was 25. In 1910 they were married. They had seven children and I'm the youngest.

The buzz went round Malvern when they were going to get married. Their wedding took place in the Lansdowne Methodist church. It was booked for a Saturday at 11 a.m. But the Minister asked them to change the time to 9 a.m. 'cos there would be too many people there to see such an unusual marriage. At 11 a.m., the roads round the church were blocked by crowds. But of course, the bride and groom had gone! The crowds felt cheated.

My father was a very strong man. He worked for different builders. He helped to build the new railway tunnel from Malvern to Ledbury in 1926. James Carty had the honour to be chosen by the Malvern gang for the "Shake Hands Ceremony", when both sets of workmen met in the middle. That was because he had worked on the tunnel from the beginning.

He had a Caribbean accent, of course. He would say "Dis and dat"—more so if he got excited. He was a good dad. Not one of us was smacked. My parents ruled with words of encouragement.

My father integrated himself into the community and he was very well liked. If my school friends had a row with me, they would tell me to go back to my own country. But our family mixed in well.

My eldest sister, Mona, was the beauty of the family. She had very tight "Astrakhan" hair. She was 5 feet 7 and elegant. At the ages of 16 and 17, she was called to sit as a model at the School of Art. Two French artists wanted her to sit nude, from the waist up. But my father heard about it and stopped it dead! She sat for Clem Walton, the photographer, too. We used to pass his studio in Court Road, on our way to school, and see her photos in his window."

Ellen Hymas told me: "The Carty boys were tall, slim and very lissom."

Alma Longstaff confirmed this. "My two brothers were famous for dancing. The local girls used to fight over them to dance with them in the Winter Gardens in Malvern. A lady said to me the other day, 'I was a dancing partner of Alec Carty who was 6 feet 3.'"

James Carty retained his charm and West Indian ways. "He was always humming a tune," said his daughter. "There was a looseness in the way he moved. He was domesticated and washed up at home. He was a very clean man and dressed smartly for Sundays. He would polish our shoes or whiten our canvas shoes. And he was always polite to people, saying 'Sir' or 'Ma'am'.

Coming from a family of 13 children, he never went to school in Barbados. I have been three times in recent years to Barbados, to see the island of my father. I felt I was walking in my father's footsteps as it is a small island. But it was a strange feeling to be there."

Francis Bird of Poolbrook recalled: "Jimmy Carty was a wonderful man. He was as strong as an ox. He was in the Malvern Male Voice Choir. His eldest sons, Alec and Gerald, became policemen in Coventry. And all the boys played football for Barnards Green.

We used to like to listen to Jimmy Carty speaking, 'cos he had a West Indian accent. He was thoroughly liked in Malvern. Wherever he went, he was a perfect gentleman."

6 ~ He Survived the Titanic!

• •

I was indeed fortunate to find and record the "Titanic" memories of Mr. Elston Crump. I met him in December 1986 when he was in Clanmere Nursing Home, Great Malvern. He was then aged about 91, he said.

He recalled: "I was born in Brixham, Devon. I was working on cruise liners from a boy. I lived in Southampton and worked in first-class cabins at times.

My father was a seaman, but not as I was. He was a trawlerman, and they went to sea in small boats to catch fish. They brought the fish back to Brixham or Southampton. Fishing is a dying trade. As a young boy, in Brixham, I would go up the steps to Berry Head to watch ships going to sea and coming into harbour. That's how I got the taste for ships—no doubt about that!

The Cunard Line were your masters. Voyages were arranged prior to our joining the ship. I liked New York. At that time, it was a very busy port. I did not go to South Africa. Africa was served by London ships.

I was 17 or 18 when I started work on the TITANIC as a steward. It was a beautiful ship, particularly at that time. There weren't many large ships then. The ballroom was nice. Chandeliers? Oh crikey, yes! and an orchestra, quite a big orchestra. I watched the dancing for a while. But I had work to do. I was detailed as to what I should look for and attend to at the time.

36

They made a swimming pool by moving articles of furniture. The food was good—the best! Certainly, better than at home.

That night of the disaster, in April 1912, on the fourth night at sea, they gave us a warning. We had to help the passengers as much as we could. We just did what we were asked to do. I did not have to swim—some did. It was cold enough as it was. It's questionable that we considered the cold. We just got on with the job. Such was the excitement that one forgot other things. We hadn't time to think. We accepted help from very many vessels. I personally at the time did not know the name of the ship that came to our rescue. They took us to New York.

The individuals I remember most of all were passengers by the name of Gould. They were American, but not what you might call "naturalised" Americans. They hadn't been there long. They were quite well off. But we did not consider that. Rich or poor, we just helped them that night. It was all a great shock.

After this experience, I still went back to being a steward. On our cruise ships, quite a few notabilities came aboard. We only contacted them in the Saloon or in the cabins. There were some famous actors, but I don't remember their names. But mostly at that time, it was notable businesspeople. There was good entertainment on board. There would be a theatre on board and plays and a lovely band.

As for the TITANIC experience—one loses sight of the event in question, purposely. You like to forget it."

Gwen Forster had a memory of the TITANIC. As a girl in 1912, she lived in Weston-Super-Mare. She told me: "In 1912, the Transatlantic Cable came into Weston-Super-Mare from America up the Bristol Channel. It was through the

Transatlantic Cable office that we, in Weston-Super-Mare, were the first to hear the tragic news of the sinking of the TITANIC. Home radio and television had not been invented then!

Two years later, in 1914, I was going down onto the Promenade one morning. Then I found I couldn't go on to the seashore because the whole place had been barricaded up with barbed wire. We were at war with Germany. The army were afraid that the enemy would attack and disrupt that same Transatlantic Cable."

Note: It is estimated that about 1,500 people died in the Titanic disaster and that about 700 people survived.

7 ~ Old Days, Old Ways

"Everybody was so happy then, before World War Two, with simpler things and a quieter life," exclaimed Peter Treherne, looking back nostalgically.

"You could go out and leave your door unlocked, in the 1920's", said Ivy Pitt, of West Malvern, "and no one would dare to enter. If anyone wasn't very well or having a baby, you would visit them and say, 'Can we help you?'"

But people were also less tolerant, as George "Divvy" Davis remembered. "My mother used to say, 'There's a couple living in a row of houses down there, and they're living in *sin!*' I was just a boy and I said to my mother, 'What do that mean, then?' And it was considered dreadful in them days."

"Divvy" Davis continued, "A policeman lived at the end of the Wells. He would meet the policeman who belonged to the Wyche here. They knew every boy and every family. And it was a disgrace to see a policeman going in somebody's house. It would be the talk of the village!"

Margaret Hands recalled her grandmother. "She came from Pendock, and she came to live with us as a widow. In those days they wore very long skirts. She would make all her own clothes—all her skirts and blouses. She used to wear boots. I never remember seeing her legs."

Colin Cutler told me: "The old black-and-white cottage in the middle of Malvern Link was built in the 1600's and was part of the Madresfield estate. It was a gamekeeper's cottage. We found a number of donkey shoes and horseshoes in the garden. When we unblocked the inglenook, we found an oven for making bread at the side of the fireplace. And inside were some very, very old leather shoes."

PUBS

"I lived in the Lower Dingle, West Malvern," said Jack Lewis, "just below the Brewers Arms. There must have been far more drunkenness then. I remember seeing drunken men sleeping on the bank above the pub. It was just accepted then."

The Lamb Inn, West Malvern, was known as The Happy Jack's Beerhouse, from 1839 to the 1850's. Then it was re-named The Lamb. The present Landlord has revived the original name *inside* the present pub. He told me it was once a farmhouse, and cattle were kept on the ground floor, level with the street.

GYPSIES

Gypsies were a common sight in the 1920's and '30's. Freda Morris recalled: "In our field in Malvern Link was a gypsy, old Lady Smith. There were half a dozen different families there, and all related to her. She paid the rent every week in a gold sovereign. Her youngest daughter, Polly, was married at the Link church. She had a red carpet right the way out to the taxi, and her wedding dress was all lace.

But when Lady Smith died, everything went wrong. They were true Romanies, you see. But they married outside and started fighting. We had to tell them to clear off.

When I took the horses down to that field, I used to go straight into Lady Smith's lovely caravan. One day, she said, 'Here is a present for you.' They were beautiful, embroidered sheets. 'You keep them. Perhaps I'll have them later on.' But when she died, everything of hers was destroyed—burnt, as is their custom."

Dorothy Jones told me: "A little gypsy lady danced for us with her tambourine. She had coloured ribbons from her waist. She asked me 'Do you think your mother would let me have a needle and thread? Some of my ribbons have come loose.' So, Mum sent up by me two reels of cotton, white and black. And the gypsy sat down and stitched on her ribbons."

CLASS DISTINCTION

David Burley tells of the social distinction that existed in his grandfather's time in Malvern: "When my grandfather first opened his Hairdressing shop in 1920, he discovered that under his predecessor, the Gentlemen's department was in two sections. There was the first Class Salon, where you walked in off the street. But if you were a working man, you had to go to the Second Class Salon which was down the side and underneath the shop.

In the first Class Salon, there was a grating between the chairs, against the wall. All the hair was swept into this grating. It fell into a bin down below, in the Second Class Salon. So, my grandfather very soon got rid of all that! But that was the social distinction at that time.

And that's why Trinity Church at Link Top was built in Victorian times. Quarries were started on the hills. The Priory people didn't want the quarry workers coming into the Priory.

So, Trinity Church was built for the quarrymen and their families."

Disney Reynolds, however, noticed class distinction in Trinity Church too, seventy years later. "Some very wealthy people came to Trinity, including Mrs. Dyson Perrins. On one side of the church, all the seats were labelled and reserved for wealthy persons and their families. But for evening service, it was a different sort of people who attended.

Frances Milsom, who spent her childhood in Tenbury Wells, said: "They were very snobbish there. One Vicar of Tenbury was the nephew of the Bishop of London. This Vicar fell in love with one of the choirgirls of Tenbury church. She was only a gardener's daughter. Everyone was surprised. You had to know your place in those days.

He proposed to marry her. So, a lady of Tenbury, Mrs. Winfield Yates, had this girl to stay with her, to teach her how to behave, in the so-called higher society.

She helped this girl, Gladys Armstrong. It was in all the newspapers—'Bishop's nephew marries Tenbury gardener's daughter.' But Gladys was ever such a nice person. That Vicar and Gladys have three daughters now. They are all very beautiful."

THE GENTRY

"In the early 1900's, the gentry were very exacting in Tenbury Wells," said Frances Milsom. "Mrs. Gordon Charles of Kyre Hall, outside Tenbury, had a little carriage, pulled by a donkey. Her companion was a funny little man who had to walk by the side of her donkey, going through the main street of the town.

And everybody had to bow to her. She never got out of

her carriage. Shop people had to run outside to see what she wanted. The children had to curtsey to her if they saw her in town. We had to bow to Mrs. Winfield Yates too. **She** was the widow of an ex-army officer."

Disney Reynolds recalled: "When I went to work for Tipping and Morris, the high-class grocers in Great Malvern, it was a different world altogether. We had a different class of customer there compared to Malvern Link.

In those days, passengers from the trains came up into Great Malvern in a station cab, drawn by horses. Visitors used to stay at the Beauchamp Hotel. It was a first-class hotel. When you went in, on every day of the year, the entrance was lined with flowers going up the steps."

Mary Davis had other memories of flowers. "I visited Davenham, the home of Mrs. Dyson Perrins, for a committee meeting. It was on a dark night in winter. At the front door, a young man in livery—a footman—came to answer the door and conducted me to the drawing room. And there was this great bowl of carnations. It was an impressive sight in winter on a dark night.

You never saw flowers all the year round in the shops like we do now. Those carnations were grown in their huge greenhouse. They used to grow pineapples and bananas too. In the drawing room, Mrs. Perrins and our Secretary were sitting listening to some famous pianist."

VICTORIAN GARDENS

In Victorian times, in Malvern, people were very fond of planting shrubs and flowering trees, in parks and gardens. Some have survived to this day. The Judas tree and the Handkerchief tree (Davidia Involucrata) are in Priory Park. In old gardens everywhere are such shrubs as Vibernum Fragrans, Skymia and Garryia Eliptica, with its long tassels. Ancient cedars and pine trees abound in Malvern's parks and churchyards.

"We walked across the fields in summer to Lansdowne Methodist church," said Audrey Morgan. "There were fields all the way from Richmond Road to Lansdowne. It was lovely to hear the bells ringing."

"Lady Howard De Walden owned half West Malvern," said Jack Lewis. "And she made that carriageway all the way round the North Hill—a marvellous walk. She did that so that she could ride in her carriage on the hills."

David Burley said his grandfather, Harry Burley, remembered seeing cattle being driven through the town from Malvern Wells, to be slaughtered in a butcher's opposite the Foley Arms Hotel. The cattle, sensing their doom, tried to escape up Red Lion Bank, opposite Burley's shop.

Pam Wootton remembered how *clean* Malvern was in the early 1920's. "A man with a spiked stick was always on Link Top common picking up any litter."

FIRST WORLD WAR

'Divvy' Davis of the Wyche said: "When I was a boy during the 1914-18 war, people used to get telegrams. I was an errand boy and I used to stand on that bank up there. A telegram boy come. I would watch him. Who's he going to?

It meant to say that the soldier was reported missing and presumed dead. You fancy the tension in a family. This woman up here lost her son and her husband. And of course, *I* was in the next war. But they didn't send them telegrams then."

Doris Smith was a pupil at the Alice Ottley School, Worcester, in the First World War. "We had maps on the wall as to where the troops were in France. The French mistress, Mlle. Sabatier, got us to grow vegetables instead of flowers in the school garden. We took these to a house where there were Belgian refugees. We had window boxes in which we planted every Friday a new lot of mustard and cress. This we took to the Belgians."

Doris continued: "On 11ᵗʰ November 1918, I was on Bellevue Terrace in Malvern. I met one of our guests, opposite W.H. Smith's shop. He had been a padre in the Dardanelles. As we stood talking, the Priory bells rang out joyfully for the Armistice. I recall that vividly."

UPSTAIRS, DOWNSTAIRS

The Aldwyn Tower hotel in Great Malvern was a comfortable place to stay, with a splendid view over the town. Doris Smith recalled: "My family came to Aldwyn Tower in 1908 and stayed till 1941. My father had bought the hotel, and my mother, being one of a family of ten, was a very good housekeeper. We were Methodists, and we advertised it as a 'Methodist Home from Home'. Our guests came from Birmingham and the West Country. Some came year after year.

We had Afternoon Tea in the Drawing Room. My mother used to pour tea from a big silver urn. We children passed round the homemade scones and cakes. In summer, mother served tea in the garden.

We had maids and a very good cook. A boy cleaned the knives and the boots, and he carried up the luggage. There were four storeys but no lifts then. There were basins in each bedroom. Maids took cans of hot water up in the morning.

Breakfast was porridge, bacon and eggs, toast, and marma-lade. Lunch was cold meat and salad, and a steamed pudding. For tea, the special Welsh drop scones were a great treat. Dinner at 7 p.m. was soup, fish, or a roast. There were two or three choices of a light cold sweet on pretty dessert plates.

It was a tee-total household, but alcoholic drinks could be ordered from a shop. Our guests would say, 'Mrs. Smith keeps a very good table!'"

MALVERN LINK RAILWAY STATION

In the 1920's and '30's, the railway gave employment to many more people than today. Frank Bowers related: "When I started in 1934 at Malvern Link station as a boy of sixteen, there was a Station Master there, and his residence was at the end of the platform. There were Refreshment Rooms and two staff worked in those rooms until the 1950's. Working on Malvern Link Goods Station then, were four clerks, a typist, a Foreman, a Checker, three porters and five motor drivers.

Before my time, railway trucks loaded with granite were unloaded *by hand*—all shovelled in by hand. The men who used to do this would roll up their trousers and show the corns *on their knees,* where the shovel went, so I was told, when I was a lad. The stone they loaded was from gravel in size to four-inch stone."

LAUNDRIES

In those days of minimal machinery and few household aids, manual labour was the order of the day. Francis Bird of

Poolbrook told me: "Mrs. Cotterell had a laundry out on the common. She did the laundry for the Colleges and some of the hotels. She did it all by hand and put it on lines on the common. Nothing ever got stolen.

I used to go to Mrs. Cotterell's every night, 'cos I did the newspaper round for Granny Andrews at the shop. I fetched the papers from the railway station and my first call was Mrs. Cotterell.

She would give me a cup of soup if it was cold weather. Her house was beautifully warm. Always ironing, she was, with flat irons heated on the hobs, by her coal fire. No electric irons were invented then!"

A QUEEN IN EVERY SENSE

Freda Morris told me about her hard-working mother. Her name was Queenie Caswell. Her real name was Regina Eldezsa Mary. She was born in the Forest of Dean. 'Regina' was after the Queen. That's why she was nicknamed Queenie. Eldezsa is the name of a Greek princess.

"We were fruit, vegetables, and coal merchants. We served all the Colleges and private schools and my mother delivered to all of them. In the summer, we handled all Norbury's produce—strawberries, cherries. We were the first to have the boysenberry, which Mr. Christopher Norbury brought over from America. It's a loganberry and a blackberry crossed. We now call it a tayberry.

First of all, we had a horse and dray. Then my dad died when I was ten, and my mother took over the business. In the end, she had two lorries, a car, a jeep, and three horses and carts. My mother was a brilliant woman."

SHOPPING

In the days before supermarkets, each individual shop was of great interest to children, and family grocers gave you personal service and attention. Mary Wells remembers the old-fashioned grocer's in Malvern Link—Sammy Green's.

"It was all parcelled up while you waited. Rice in puce bags, sugar in blue bags. I used to watch Sammy Green's dexterity in getting just the right amount of rice without spilling it and making it into a square package. He had to fold the bag—no Sellotape then.

It was quite a work of art. I was intrigued as a little girl. I used to see if I could do it by practising at home. And the coffee grinding machine used to smell delightful.

I also had to do mother's shopping at Bayley's in Newtown Road. 'Will you ask for tasty cheese? And will you ask if you can taste it? Because you know what your father's like. He likes mature Cheddar'. So, as a little girl, I would ask, 'Can I have a bit to taste, like the ladies do?'"

OLD WAYS WITH FOOD

Mary Wells continued: "All my school friends were farmer's daughters. I spent every weekend with them on their farms. I went to Mill Farm, owned by the Bullocks, in Guarlford Road, where I used to ride bare-back.

They had a huge cider press there, where the apples would be thrown in, in the autumn. The cider would come out—real rough stuff—scrumpy. But we children used to drink it. It's amazing we didn't become intoxicated! Many public houses [pubs] had cider presses and also bakeries in the old days."

Ellen Hymas told me: "Mum used to skin rabbits herself. Ugh! The butcher would paunch them for her. She would hang them up to skin them. My Mum was very good at dressing fowls too."

"My mother could cut up a pig alongside any man", said Freda Morris, proudly. "We used to clean the chitlings and we had all the hams hanging up in the shop. People would buy home cured bacon—as sweet as anything. The hams would last us for twelve months. You never taste that now.

When I was eight, my mother started doing faggots and peas on a Saturday. I was given the job of going house to house. It was sixpence for two faggots and a big spoonful of pea soup. I would get old Granny Hawker's basin and run back to the shop. I must have walked

miles, really, because they wouldn't trust me with two dishes at the same time."

A FAMOUS LOCAL GARDENER

In the early 1900's, William Crump was Head Gardener at Madresfield Court, with 40 gardeners under him. He had been Head Gardener at Blenheim Palace before that.

"He produced the melon, Blenheim Orange", said Dorothy Pembridge. "He also crossed a Worcester Pearmain with a Cox's Orange, and it was called a William Crump. It had the early property of the Pearmain and the keeping quality of the Cox's. It was a very nice apple and grew in the garden at Madresfield Court winning an Award from the Royal Horticultural Society in 1908."

Audrey Morgan, as a child, recalled seeing William Crump and his wife. She said, "Mrs. Crump, in the 1920's, always wore a long black dress and a white mob cap." William Crump died in 1932, aged 89. He is buried in Madresfield churchyard.

HORSES

"When I was a child," said Dorothy Jones, "there were lots of horses and carts. People would go out into the street with their buckets and shovels 'cos the horse manure was good for the garden. In the Council fields, the men used to bring home the cart horses from the grit wagons. When those horses were unharnessed, they galloped round the fields, rolled on their backs, and kicked out. They were so pleased to be free of their heavy harness!"

Freda Morris told me a sad story about a horse. "Sam Caswell was my dad. He was known everywhere. He used to go into the market, in his pony and trap. He came home one Friday from market, and he was shaking. Mum thought he was drunk. But he died within a week. He was buried here in Malvern Link. There was 140 wreaths. St. Matthias church was packed. They were all Worcester farmers, Gloucester farmers. My father was brought to church on his own horse-drawn dray. Tommy was his horse. I wasn't allowed to attend. I was too young, you see.

The horse was put out in the paddock, and he never done a day's work after that. Twelve months to the day, he was lying down and had to be shot. He was pining for my dad. He wouldn't move. He must have known."

NO MOD. CONS.!

"I had to collect the accumulators," recalled Mary Wells, "or the radio wouldn't work! They had to be charged at the ironmonger's and they were incredibly heavy to carry. But nobody ever felt any sympathy for me! I had to trudge up from Madresfield to Barnards Green to Edwards shop. You left the accumulators there for two days, then you collected them.

My mother said, 'Don't forget to collect the accumulators tonight on your way from school 'cos Tommy Farr is fighting (a famous boxer of the day), and your father wants to hear the fight on the wireless.'"

Joy Van Daesdonk was born in Bank Cottage, Malvern Wells. She said, "We were the only people to have a toilet upstairs in the 1930's. And nobody had a bathroom except in the big houses.

We had a row of bells in the back hall, and they still worked. One was for the front door; the others were for each room in the house. Our predecessor had had a maid to answer the bells! But we had the bells taken away after the war. They would be quite a feature now.

We had gas in our cottage in the 1890's, but no electricity until 1946. Until then, we only had oil lamps."

Ellen Hymas remembered that the quarrymen in North Malvern blew a whistle at 12 noon and 4 p.m. to warn local folk about the blasting. The gaffer was Mr. Wilkins. But the quarries have now been silent for many a year. The last quarry ceased to work about 25 years ago.

Let Meriel Hodgetts sum up the tremendous changes Malvern has seen since the Second World War. "Sixty years ago, when we came to Upper Welland, old-fashioned country people were living here. Now they're mostly all incomers. It's just a dormitory, really."

8 ~ We Went to School

• •

"I was born in Stretton Grandison, Herefordshire, and went to the village school there," said Rose Nash, in Madresfield. "In winter, we had to walk by the roads—about two miles. I used to wear boots and gaiters, all buttoned up. In the summer, we could walk across the fields and hopyards, through a little spinney and down a bank.

I liked Drawing. I didn't like History, but I liked sewing and knitting, which I still do now. Mrs. Gale was the Head teacher. She was marvellous. But we used to pinch her apples! She had some lovely red ones in her garden—Desirée. But she didn't mind. She was a very good teacher."

Winifred Barnes remembered her schooldays in Malvern Link, at the school in Cromwell Road. "There were no radiators in school—just big tortoise stoves. Pupils sitting in the back desks couldn't feel any warmth whatsoever. There were no school dinners—only a glass of milk at 11 a.m. But we always came home to a hot lunch."

Margaret Davis recalled, "At Malvern Wells, we little girls all wore white pinafores. As an Infant, I had to sit at a desk and wait for my sister to accompany me home. But I was always fiddling with the inkwells. They fascinated me. The pens would roll down and splash you.

Once I got in real trouble. The ink spilt down my white pinafore. And I wondered what Mother would say. But she very kindly wasn't cross. She said, 'Oh, I'll get it out in milk. Don't worry.'"

Joan George at Malvern Wells school said: "Children walked a long way to school, along rough roads in all weathers. There were no school buses then. Children often arrived late, very wet, and muddy. Some boys had to help with farm chores before setting out for school."

HEADMASTERS AND TEACHERS

George 'Divvy' Davis related, "At Lower Wyche school, my Headmaster was P.G. Staines. And he had come out of the army. He never had no trouble, and he never used the cane. We was always playing on the common, and on the Wells Road, playing tops with these whips.

Our Headmaster said to us, "Now, when I blow the whistle, you'll have to come back, or else you won't be allowed on the road." And when he blew the whistle, *everybody* rushed up. There was discipline. The cane wasn't needed."

Ellen Hymas recalled the Headmaster at North Malvern School. "Mr. Sendall was very strict, but we all benefited from that."

"We were taught separately from the girls at North Malvern," said Disney Reynolds. "Miss Worthington was very strict with the girls. They were just like the Girls' College when they walked down the road. You daren't do anything wrong."

"I went to school at Mill Lane *College*," said Charles Smith. "Our Headmaster used to say it sounded more important, calling it a college. I never cared much for school. I was glad to get out. The best subject was Geography. I was very keen on that. The Vicar of Christchurch came into school often. He always brought his two dogs with him, and he tied them up outside."

"I went to Pickersleigh Road Council School," said Dennis Morgan "It was run on a shoestring then. Very little was spent on school equipment. When I first started, we had tin trays and silver sand. We used to draw in the sand and copy shapes of letters to learn to write. As a small pupil, I remember taking sixpence towards Miss Green's wedding present, which was a mirror to go on a mantelpiece. I was always top in Geography."

Frank Bowers remembers learning Mental Arithmetic, taught by Miss Dolly Cox, who was very, very strict. "She would put seven thimbles on her fingers. We pupils would be standing round the classroom. If we didn't answer she would tap you on the head with her thimbled fingers. You had to be quick to answer. But I've a lot to thank Dolly Cox for. It has stood me in good stead, that Mental Arithmetic."

Jim Tudge remembers Mr. Staines at Lower Wyche school. "He was a very enthusiastic teacher. We used to print our own school magazine. He played games with us on the common, which was unheard of till then.

He was great on poetry. We learnt it by heart. Every old pupil I meet from his school seems to be fond of poetry."

Nancy Clay, at school in the Herefordshire village of Tarrington, also enjoyed poetry. "We had to learn by heart, 'Horatio on the Bridge' and 'Ode to the West Wind'. 'O wild West Wind, thou breath of Autumn's being'."

SUBJECTS

Eric Jones reminisced, "All six of us went to Cowleigh School. I started at 3 years old and walked the 3 miles to school at

3 years old! I remember all Miss Andrews taught me. She must have made it interesting. She was stern but kindly. You listened. She made History and all about the ancient Empires very interesting. In those days, the globe was more than half pink with the British Empire!"

"The Reverend Isaac Williams called in every morning to take prayers. We had to learn the Commandments: 'Honour thy father and thy mother.'"

Dorothy Jones, at school in Somers Park Road, loved English. "I loved Nature stories and Nature poems. I liked making up poetry. Miss Evans read out to the class the stories I had written."

Frances Milsom, at school in Tenbury Wells, said, "Our teacher was very keen for us to hear Lamb's Tales from Shakespeare. They weren't quite so hard to learn as the actual plays.

In summer, we used to sit on the Headmistress's lawn to do sewing. We made her some curtains once—all hand sewn, with drawn thread work."

Minna Bowers remembered Needlework at the Girls' Grammar School in Worcester. "Miss Steele, our Headmistress, taught Needlework. We had to make a camisole—a bodice. It combined all the samples of stitches and seams. It had tucks, lace, and tiny little buttonholes. Later on, we made a Cookery apron and sleeves and a Science overall. And the teacher would read to us if it was a quiet lesson."

"I took first prize in the Cookery class", exclaimed Joan Preece. "We had a fully equipped kitchen in our school in Pickersleigh Road. I used my mother's recipe: Breadcrumbs in the bottom, dry bits of cheese, milk, and a little bit of butter—and put it in the oven. Believe me, it was delicious. And that is what I had first prize for! They taught us to make Welsh cakes and shortbread. One day we done some pancakes. We used to eat half of them before we got home!

And we done Laundry as well, but not much time to get things dry. I had the brainy idea of putting my friend's cardigan, which I had washed, into the school oven to dry, and when the oven was on. She took it home with a big scorch mark on it. I said to her, only the other day, "Do you remember what your Mum said about that?!"

And we had to take pillowcases and handkerchiefs to iron, to learn to press properly. No electric irons then—only flat irons."

"Games in the playground?" said Nancy Clay. "Hopscotch and skipping. Whips and tops. Hoops. Keeping house, with tins and pieces of china."

"We played Sheep, Sheep Come Home in two lines," said Ellen Hymas, "the one in the middle tried to catch us. The boys played marbles. After the first world war, there was an old tank on Link Top. Children played on top of it. 'Keep the pot boiling'."

"Country Dancing and Folk Dancing were very popular when I was at school at Somers Park Road," enthused Dorothy Jones. "Mr. Powell encouraged us to enjoy music and dancing. We specialised in the Flamborough Sword Dance. The Link School did the Ribbon Dance, round the Maypole, with the May Queen and her attendants."

DRAMA AND MUSIC

Joy Van Daesdonk went to school at Link Lodge, Malvern Link, at Miss Burgess's Queen Anne High School. "We did

Hiawatha once. I was Minnehaha because I had two long plaits. On the whole, girls had short hair then."

Ellen Hymas remembered a Christmas play at North Malvern School. "I was the plum pudding. Phyllis Calder was the Christmas cake. I wore a big round frame draped in black and brown, with yellowy spots on it for the fruit. Phyllis wore white and pink for the cake icing. I thought she looked very pretty."

Margaret Hands recalled the Schools Music Festival held annually in the Winter Gardens. "We were in the school choir. Our Headmaster, Mr. Powell was very good at music. He was a perfectionist with his school choir.

Once, we beat the Malvern Girls' College. We had a trophy for that. One of the songs was 'Tiger, Tiger, Burning Bright'. We were so chuffed that we had beaten the Malvern Girls' College."

Francis Bird was taught other skills at school. "George Mooney was a very good chess player. He would take on the whole class at chess. He would look over the top of his glasses and tell you what next move to make, without getting up from his desk.

Mr. Hayward played the violin and taught children to play. It cost us sixpence a lesson. We bought our violins for 30 shillings, paying a shilling a week to buy them. Some of Mr. Hayward's pupils continued playing violin or cello into adult life."

PUNISHMENTS

"At my school in Guarlford," said Frank Burston, "the teachers were more strict than today. Everyone looked up to them. It didn't do us any harm to have the cane—which I did quite often."

"I've only once had the cane," said Arthur Russell. "Someone left the tap on in the school washroom. As nobody would confess, we **all** had the cane!"

"I was punished by cane for playing truant," confessed Disney Reynolds. "Six stripes. There it was in the logbook. Mr. Sendall was a hard man, but he kept everything in order. In those days, we were frightened of a policeman."

Girl pupils did not escape punishment. "We all got the cane once," said Margaret Hands. "We had stopped to look at a fire and a fire engine. We had forgotten all about the time and we were late for school. So Mr. Powell gave us all the cane—even the girls, on our palms."

And parents supported the teachers over punishments. "I accepted the cane many times," commented Francis Bird. "If you told your mother you'd had the cane, she would say, "Serves you right!""

Dennis Morgan was philosophical about discipline in school. "I had the cane many times—sometimes justly, sometimes unjustly. It learned you that life wasn't always quite fair. Today, with all this attention, it removes people's responsibility. They all become wimps in the end, 'cos they need somebody to sort out their problems for them. I think the old system was far better for character building."

"I played truant once," confided Arthur Russell. "My friend, Arthur George and myself went up to St. James's Road and stayed out of sight. My father had a chicken house, and several mornings I've hidden myself in there and waited for the school bell to stop ringing. But I was caught out in the end.

We used to have a post on a Sunday. A letter came from the headmaster and my mother read it out loud. It said I hadn't been to school on a certain day. There was nothing wrong with school. Arthur and I just felt like a holiday!"

UNUSUAL SCHOOL MEMORIES

Some Malvern folks remember their schools for unusual reasons. Gwen Forster said, "Until we came to Malvern in 1918, we lived in Weston-Super-Mare. I went to Rossholm School there and we played hockey on the sands."

The Lyttelton Grammar School in Great Malvern provided choristers for Malvern Priory. Jack Lewis has vivid memories of being a pupil there. "I started there at nearly nine years old. My parents were musical. I was very soon in the Priory choir. If you did well in the choir, your school fees went down and down.

The first lesson of the day was from 9 o'clock 'till 9:45—choir practice. It was almost like a cathedral in a way. The choirboys went to the Choir Room. I enjoyed that side of it.

There were only two masters there. The Headmaster, George Thornton, took the older boys. He taught everything—History, Geography, Algebra, and Languages. My father had been at school there before me. *He* did bookkeeping early in the century. And you could do Shorthand too then. But there were no specialist teachers.

I went there in early 1925. The first time I took books home for homework, my father looked at them and said, 'Oh, those are the *same* books I used to have!' The school had become fossilised. And it was under the *same* Headmaster too!

My fellow pupils came from the Malverns and the surrounding countryside. They were tradespeople's sons mostly. I lived at the top end of West Malvern above the church. There was only one way to get to Great Malvern—and that was over the hill! Every day—up and over! Up the valley and down the other side. It took twenty minutes. That was because we were late all the time. We ran down past St. Ann's Well. But it took much longer coming back at night."

Mary Davis has happy memories of the old Ledbury Grammar School. "We lived in Colwall. I got a Scholarship to Ledbury Grammar School. Me and my sister went there to school when it opened in 1923. I got 99% for French that first term as I had learned some French in my private school beforehand.

The school was housed in Ledbury Hall. It was a wonderful building, with beautiful wood floors and carved staircases. We used to play cricket on the big lawn. There was a shrubbery. We had a netball pitch on the tennis court which had belonged to the house. The lodges were occupied by caretakers. What had been the stables was made into a gymnasium. The teaching was good. It's only when you're older that you realise these things."

Elsie Jennings went to St. Joseph's Roman Catholic school in Newtown Road. "We had three women teachers. They were all Irish. Miss Kyle used to tell us ghost stories on some afternoons. The Irish are very like that, aren't they?"

Helen Mooney remembered her schooling at the City of Worcester Secondary School for Girls. "I was there from 1919 to 1925. Miss Steele was my Headmistress. She was a very remote person. You just kept away from her.

Miss Tyers, our Music teacher, was great on music. Every summer term we had the grand concert at the Public Hall, with the Prizegiving. We sang lots of songs, many in three parts. Miss Tyers taught Music and French. She scared me stiff! She was the centre of music for Worcester. She had played in an ensemble with Elgar conducting."

SPECIAL EVENTS

Bill Sims went to Guarlford High School, next to the church, until the age of 14, in 1920. Bill remembers that there were from 70 to 90 pupils in school then. The highlight of the school year was the Summer Outing to the Old Hills, where the children had sports and a tea party. The journey there was made in a harvest wagon, belonging to Mr. Bradshaw, who farmed at Guarlford Court Farm.

In the 1920's every school celebrated Empire Day on 24th May, annually. Disney Reynolds told me, "We used to sing a song:

We salute thee and we pray
God to bless our land today …

Frances Milsom's schooldays were spent in Tenbury Wells. "We went to church once a week from school. On Ascension Day we had to be up very early to see the primroses and wild-flowers in the countryside.

In Tenbury Wells, there were little local Eistedfodds. All the schoolchildren had to make a garment for an exhibition. One year I won a prize for a nightdress I'd made … and there were concerts."

As a schoolgirl, Dorothy Jones remembered celebrating the Silver Jubilee of King George V and Queen Mary in 1935. "We had sports in the field. Each child was given a cardboard box with a tea in it—a bun, a cake, a sandwich, a glass of squash. And we were given a special Jubilee mug. My twin sisters had a Coronation mug for George VI in 1937."

We will finish with a nostalgic memory from Minna Bowers about a favourite teacher known to generations of pupils at the Girls' Grammar School in Worcester. "Miss Glover was a lovely woman. She was very kind, especially to the first-year girls. She rode a high bicycle and lived in Bevere. I shall always remember her sympathetic tone of voice when she would say, 'I'm *afraid* you must have a Disorder Mark.' She was so sorry to have to do it!"

9 ~ Top of the Class

Malvern has long been famous for its colleges and independent schools, offering education of the highest calibre:

MALVERN COLLEGE founded in 1865

MALVERN GIRLS' COLLEGE founded in 1893

ST. JAMES'S founded in 1902

LAWNSIDE founded in about 1857 and joined
St. James's in 1994

THE ABBEY founded in 1880 and merged with
St. James's in 1979

MALVERN COLLEGE

The College opened in 1865. It was one of the 'Railway' Colleges, created in the wake of the growing network of railways in the 1860's. The railway came to Malvern in 1859.

Here are some revealing extracts from the College's Centenary book, AGE FRATER (title of the School Song in Latin), edited by George Sayer.

First Impressions—from various old boys

The first thing that struck me was the very happy atmosphere of the place. The House had suddenly turned from a bleak prison into a lively and jolly little place. Boys came up to us and asked us why we looked so mournful. I expected to be pushed out of the way and hurled into stone walls. But no, people said sorry if they bumped into me.

My first impression of the school was of magnitude and freedom.

I thought the College buildings looked dark and unhomely. The buildings seemed to jump at one as I came down the drive. They were more like a rather strong castle, built in the neo-Gothic style.

The first thing I noticed was the hills. They seemed to tower right over the school. I wasn't sure whether I was going to enjoy myself here.

I found the wide, draughty corridors of the main building strangely frightening. But the dark passages of my House I found friendly and warm.

I found the walking to and fro in the large grounds to be tiring, but now I've got used to it.

The motto of Malvern College is *SAPIENS QUI PROSPICIT* (He is wise who looks to the future). These Latin words also appear on the label of Crawford's Old Scotch Whisky, which the first Headmaster, The Revd. Arthur Faber (a Scot), liked to drink.

In contrast, the Coat of Arms of Malvern College empha-sises **water**—the blue, wavy water of three Malvern wells: Holy-well, St. Ann's, and the Chalybeate. The chevrons symbolise the Malvern Hills and the red circles represent the Diocese of Worcester.

George Chesterton described the Centenary of the College in 1965. "It was a very well-planned occasion lasting a week. The Queen Mother came on the last day. Harold Macmillan came too but he was not prime minister then."

More Old Pupils Remember

My prospective Housemaster was human. I had imagined he would be a fierce old man but I was wrong. He wore a smile.

Work

Having been told that Malvern College did no work but only played games, I was dumbfounded by the work we had to do.

Prefects

On the first Sunday of term, it amused me greatly to see College Prefects with long tails and silver topped canes. It's a pity those are going to be abolished. The Prefects were very, very powerful people. They carried *their* boaters in their hands. Because there was nobody to tell *them* to wear them on their heads.

Advice to House Prefects

"It will help a House Prefect very much if he is a good games player. Playing games is a most important part of House Spirit. The games player will usually find it easier to control and have the respect of the rowdier members. A sense of humour and the gift of repartee are important qualities."

A Day in the Life of a Sixth Form Boy (undated)

The corridor is cold and long. Breakfast consists of hot tea and heavy porridge. Conversation is often perfunctory at school if it is not trivial or obscene: this is because you know everyone too well.

The dormitory contains a bleak revealing light, which emphasizes its chilliness. The classroom is large and cold. There are only seven of us waiting for the master. Today, he is wearing white socks. These fascinate me. During the next class, I dream of girls.

Lunch is a garrulous, unnourishing meal. On the top table, the Housemaster sits, surrounded by masters and sheepish prefects. The Chaplain is here today, and I must talk about religion, or perhaps fishing. One master has retreated into a chewing silence. I can't blame him.

I am playing centre-half this afternoon. At half-time, I look up at the school buildings, square and unmovable. They seem to have grown out of the hillside. They have the same mossy greyness as the mother rock.

Food (by a Housemaster)

School diet had to be supplemented by well-stocked tuckboxes and continual shopping at the Grub. Potted paste (now upgraded and known as pâté) on toast, would scarcely be acceptable today as a cooked supper. But it did not seem outrageous then, when it was the custom to take food at least *six* times a day:

Breakfast in Houses

Break—coffee and buns at the Grub

Lunch

A snack after lunch

House tea or poached eggs and sausages at the Grub
Supper
After Prayers—cocoa and biscuits or soup and bread

Cross-Country Running

This is a minor sport that is booming. It used to be confined
to the Ledbury Run in the Easter term. This is still a splendid
event. The boys run for the love of running and for the personal
triumph of being able to run from Ledbury at a fair pace and
over the Malvern Hills.

Fagging

In my House, we prefects very nearly abolished personal fagging
a year ago. We thought it would be good for us to brush our
own clothes and clean our *own* shoes. What, however, decided
us to keep fagging, was the personal relationship, which we
thought was almost always valuable.

Reminiscences About the Railway
(which skirts the College grounds)

Those were the days of vast double-headed Sunday excursion
trains from the Black Country. They rested in Malvern Wells
siding until it was time to slide down and take up the day-trip-
pers, now footsore, hot and dis-illusioned, after trailing straight
up and down the Malvern Hills.

The main line Hereford to Paddington was served, for
the most part, by gleaming Hall-class engines; occasionally, a
Castle came through. During cricket matches, the variety of
railway traffic added interest for spectators and fielders alike.

One remembers, on sunny days, great clouds of smoke and
steam, as passenger trains blustered up the gradient towards

the tunnel; and earth tremors as the spirited drivers thundered down. There were goods trains of unbelievable length.

After dark, one could glimpse cosy-looking compartments and fancy oneself on the way home at the end of term. Sometimes, in the small hours, eerie duets could be heard from engines on heavy goods trains.

Today, the Diesels with their throbbing turbines, asthmatic wheezing's, and vulgar horns provide a different sort of background music. Though much of the glamour and character has been lost, at least the railway line is ***alive.***

George Sayer taught at Malvern College for over 30 years and was Head of the English Department. He said, "I was a pupil of C.S. Lewis, who had been a pupil at Malvern College and had disliked it. I introduced his teaching methods in my work here.

Among my old pupils is Jeremy Paxman. He was one of my pupils who became a permanent friend of mine. That's one of the nicest experiences for a schoolmaster, when pupils become life-long friends. Jeremy comes to see me occasionally. He's a household name now as a presenter and interviewer on radio and television."

The Army Cadet Force (ACF)

Wilfred Hoskins told me, "I arrived in Malvern in October 1960. I was employed by the College as a staff instructor for the Army Cadet Force. When I came here, the College boys had to wear boaters. There was an element in Malvern that used to take the mickey out of them. One day, a College boy got beaten up in Priory Park and nobody went to help the boy.

I had been in the Marines—in the Commandos. I taught

the boys unarmed combat. I showed some of the Senior Prefects the tricks of the trade. And after about three months, the College boys were left alone because they could be very nasty now, when they were upset!

The police wouldn't do anything, so they did it themselves. They managed to walk along the streets with boaters on. And nobody tipped the boaters over their eyes. They got treated with respect, as everybody should be.

It was compulsory then for every boy to be in one of the Cadet Forces. There was the Naval section and the RAF section. I was in charge of the army one. We camped some weekends in the Brecons. I did that for twelve years. All the public schools did this at that time. And many of the state schools too. We used to meet them at shooting matches.

For equipment we had two ancient canons. They were used in the 1920's when the college had horses for pulling mowers to cut grass. On Wednesday afternoons, the horses pulled the guns around the College instead. But that was before my time."

George Chesterton recalled those ancient guns. "They were nine pounder muzzle loading guns dating from the Crimean war and were housed in the Gun Shed. The horses which pulled the guns were loaned by Mr. Jones, a local coal merchant.

On one famous occasion, when a number of cadet forces paraded in Marlborough High Street, with Malvern as the only artillery unit taking the 'right of line', it began to rain heavily. Mr. Jones insisted that his horses should be covered. Much to Malvern's chagrin the covers bore in large white letters: JONES BROS, COAL MERCHANT."

Sport

"Before the war (World War II) George Chesterton, one of

69

the Housemasters, was the demon speed bowler for Worcestershire," said Wilfred Hoskins.

"When they played Rugby football at Rugby School, it was a blood match. Rugby were our greatest rivals. We used to send our army cadet signalman with the team to Rugby with his radio. And he would relay back to us a commentary on the match coming direct from Rugby.

And there were plenty of other sports. The College boys played golf at the Wells golf course. They went sailing on the Severn not far from Upton. They rode at the Avenue Riding Stables. They were taught canoeing in the College swimming pool, and they learnt how to do the Eskimo roll. They had wonderful weekends on the rivers. We would take them to Brecon, nip down Gloucester way and wait for them to come down to us on the River Severn."

The Chapel

It was opened in 1899. The side extension was erected in 1908 when the number of pupils increased. It was also referred to as "The Rabbit Hutches"—and still is!

"Oh! The 'Rabbit Hutches'!" exclaimed Wilf Hoskins. "That is where the Junior school go. Eighteen little boys to a bench are crammed in there. They had to keep their elbows in!"

A Royal Guard of Honour

"I organised a Royal Guard of Honour for the Queen Mother at the Centenary," announced Wilf Hoskins proudly. "And I had to do something to *sell* the Guard of Honour to the Queen Mother. So, I put a little black boy in the front row. I warned him what was going to happen. I knew the Queen Mother would want to have a go at him—and she did! He was ever so pleased. He was from Nigeria. His father was a very important fellow.

The Queen Mother spoke to me. She asked me if we had ever met. I said, "Not at close quarters. I was on the cruiser Berwick, and you were on another warship when you went to New York".

Back to this little Nigerian boy. One day he saw snow for the first time. He was rolling in it! I grabbed him by the scruff of the neck and hoisted him up. He said, "I've heard of snow and seen pictures of it, but I've never felt it."

I had to explain to him, "All this snow on your clothes—when you go somewhere warm, that snow is going to melt. And then you're going to get sopping wet." And he said, "I didn't know. Nobody has told me that."

He was a nice little kid. He left school, went back to Nigeria and they dragged him into the Civil war there. And he was killed in a few weeks. In those days there would be about half-a-dozen boys from overseas. And they were very timid. The coloured boys found it very difficult in the cold winter."

The Second World War

George Chesterton, as a pupil at Malvern College in 1939, has vivid memories of the College being moved to Blenheim Palace for a year. The College buildings were destined for the Admiralty—but *they* went to Bath instead!

"A ball had just been held at Blenheim Palace for 1500 people. The extra kitchens were still there and came in useful for feeding the College boys. Huts were hastily built for them as classrooms. The dormitories were in state rooms. Coconut matting had been put down on floors, and interior walls were protected by boarding up to six feet. The statues had blankets over them.

We had our own Home Guard to patrol the grounds at night. The boys took it in turns to do fire-watching. They patrolled the four-and-a-half-acre roof and the grounds. It was all great fun!"

College Pranks

George Sayer recalled, "It was a fashion at one time for Senior boys to break out of their dorms at night to invade the rooms of masters, especially Housemasters. It didn't do any harm. They might have smoked cigarettes. We spent a long time trying to catch these boys—but we failed! They would get into unlocked rooms in masters' private houses.

But what happened was that one master would catch another master, thinking he was a boy! Quite easily done—at night! We called it 'The Burglaries'. I think it was rather fun. But I was never a Housemaster."

Wilf Hoskins added, "At the end of the summer term, the jokers used to perform. They would empty all the dustbins on the cricket pitch.

They climbed up the College clock and put gloves on the hands. They must have gone over the top, on a rope, 'cos we taught them abseiling. But I never taught them to go up there.

Did you hear about the statue of St. George? One day he looked as if he had German measles. He was covered in these little white round stickers. You put them round a hole in your file to reinforce the paper. He had thousands of those all over him. And *he* is the College War Memorial!

Mr. Lace, who was an old boy, went stark raving mad. The workshop people had to come immediately and put a fence round him and go up and clean all these spots off him. That had been done at night.

In the end, things got so bad they had to have masters patrolling the grounds at night. On the last day of term—that's when the devilment takes place—especially the summer term."

Here is Wilf Hoskin's final nostalgic comment: "My time at the College was far better than my time in the Marines. I was at the College 25 years, till I was 65. My face fitted. I got on well with everybody there."

Epilogue—Girls at Malvern College.

There were no girls at Malvern College when George Sayer was teaching English there. Today, girls *are* present as pupils in large numbers. George Sayer commented wryly: "I think it's very good for boys! Girls have a civilising effect on boys, just as women have on men. I really believe this. But I'm not at all certain that boys are good for girls!"

MALVERN GIRLS' COLLEGE

Malvern Girls' College was founded by Miss Poulton and Miss Greenslade in 1893. From 1899, the school was housed in Ivydene Hall, Albert Road South. Ivydene is still today the oldest boarding house of the College.

The attic in Ivydene with its William Morris wallpaper slept eleven servants in 1913. One of the 'tweenies' ('between maids') who was there came from Rous Lench, near Evesham. She had arrived by train. She remembered hearing and seeing the trains passing through Great Malvern station. This made her homesick because she wanted to travel home on them.

Today's Main Building of Malvern Girls' College was the Imperial Hotel, built in 1862, next door to Great Malvern station. Still resembling a French chateau, it was the most prestigious of Malvern's Water Cure hotels.

Pamela Hurle, in her Centenary History of Malvern Girls' College, has this to say: "The admissions books of the College for the early 20th century offer some commentary on social life then. Only the affluent could afford to educate their daughters privately. One father had stated that his daughter was to be prepared for life in India, by the time she was 18. Her education must equip her 'to rule a large household'".

Phyllis Castle was a pupil at Malvern Girls' College from 1921 to 1925. "I had a governess for quite a long time in Cheltenham, where we lived," she said. "Then I came to The Mount house at M.G.C., and our Headmistress was Miss Kate Dawson. She was very nice.

Miss Poulton and Miss Greenslade had retired from teaching by then, so we didn't see much of them. But we still used to see Miss Poulton going round, looking after the maintenance of the buildings, and boarding houses. She and Miss Greenslade had a parrot in their front window. He was very noisy if you had to go to their door!

It was a very cloistered life. Our parents would visit us twice a term. But we were not allowed home at all in the term—there was no half-term! The Seniors would shop in the lunch hour 1 to 2 p.m. I never knew where the Boys' College was. But we used to see them walking past.

Malvern was still very Victorian back then. Like all the spa towns it was rather snobbish. We saw very few people and there weren't many day girls then.

I remember an Indian girl student at College. She was the first to come here. You didn't see a lot of Chinese girls like you see now. This Indian girl was Dorothy Diaz. She's still on the

Old Girls' list, I see. She wore a sari, which was very unusual, and her sari was in our school colours, which were navy with a border of maroon. Dorothy Diaz had to have a fire in her room as a special favour. On seeing her in her sari, some Malvern people questioned her: "Are you a Christian?" Now they are quite used to seeing veiled Moslem girl students here!"

Peggy Edwards, who was a pupil in 1912, and was also in The Mount boarding house, recalls: "Doorstep bread and butter was served for tea, and boiled milk was served four times a day. For meals, there was always milk pudding. We also had boiled puddings such as "spotted baby" or "treacle baby", except on Sunday, when we had white blancmange and stewed fruit."

Phyllis Castle added, "We dreaded to see the Mac Fisheries van arriving. Cod seemed to be the cheapest fish in those days. It was not so long after the First World War, so some things were still scarce."

But Phyllis and her schoolmates did enjoy the picnics in the Games field in summer. "And we had a picnic at the British Camp on the hills. A charabanc took us there. We climbed the Beacon 'cos it was the only place where we were allowed to buy ginger beer in the little cafe on top.

We were certainly not allowed to eat in the street. Pocket money was restricted to £1 a term. There was nothing to spend it on. So, I even took some money back home. There was no tuck shop. Our sweets were doled out to us on Sundays."

Peggy Edwards also recalled picnics in the playing field. "There was a hay party and a picnic tea when it was cut. A horse called Charley was kept for mowing the tennis courts. He was quite partial to a tasty bit of school hat—the old boater variety, if anyone had left one on the palings round the pavilion."

Barbara Brown began as a pupil at Malvern Girls' College

in 1917, at the age of nine. She recalled, "Every Ascension Day we went, in charabancs, to the British Camp for a picnic. And every Saturday evening, the Middle School and the Seniors had dancing together."

"On Saturday mornings we did Art or Music," said Phyllis Castle. "We watched the matches played and we used to swim a lot in the College pool.

On Sundays, we all went to the Priory wearing white costumes in summer and black stockings. It was navy-blue in winter and navy-blue hats with house colours as bands. Often the Priory service was followed by the Litany, for another twenty minutes—and we couldn't escape! We had to sit in the side aisle and could see nothing. Back at school, we had to write home twice a week.

The only outside work we, as Seniors did, was to run a Cub pack at St. Peter's Orphanage in West Malvern. And we would take those little boys for a walk. That was very popular."

In 1925, Miss Greenslade purchased the 11-hole golf course on the Malvern Wells common, together with the former Golf House. Girls would take a train from Great Malvern Station to the station then at Malvern Wells—three pence return, for their golf lessons.

Peggy Edwards had a story to tell about the parrot that belonged to Miss Poulton and Miss Greenslade. "In the window of their study, Pierrot the parrot had his cage. In the summer, he would be brought into the garden. I, with others, spent time trying—without any success whatever—to teach him to say 'Damn!' Pierrot refused to be educated in a girls' school!"

Miss Iris Brooks was a formidable and powerful Head-mistress. She reigned for 26 years—from 1928 to 1954. Ken

Lynes, who was Houseman at Malvern Girls' College for 43 years remembers her well.

"She was a very stern person. Miss Brooks was like the Queen—stately in her long black gown. If workmen were working on the ground floor during Assembly and Prayers, once Prayers were over, her secretary would run in front and usher the workmen out before Miss Brooks appeared. And all the girls used to line the walls if visitors or staff came past. But now it's not so strict.

The teacher's desk used to be on a platform, raised above the class. But now, they've got to be *with* the girls—on their level. So new desks came in, Formica-topped. We Housemen used to have to fill inkwells. Then the biro came in, didn't it?"

Malvern's independent schools have always employed numerous local people as domestic staff, groundsmen, and gardeners, as did the water cure establishments before them. Down in the basement of the former Imperial Hotel even today, there is still the feeling of a hotel, with the little workrooms and laundry rooms off the long corridors.

As Houseman, and later Head Houseman, Ken Lynes was responsible for a wide variety of daily tasks. He saw many changes during his time at the College.

"In 1951 we used to make mattresses for the girls' beds", said Ken Lynes. "All the flock was carded on a machine. I suppose it was cheaper to make them, with seamstresses present. Miss Jarrett was Head Seamstress and she had five women under her for repairs and alterations.

The Housemen stuffed the mattresses and walled them to make them firm, then buttoned them. And the women sewed them. We re-upholstered chairs too. Eventually, the College started *buying* mattresses.

There were four laundresses at the College in those days. The little girls were younger then. They started at 5 years old. And the Housemen in the boarding houses cleaned their shoes.

There were a lot of Welsh maids at MGC then. They lived on the top floor of the old hotel. Those rooms are now Music Rooms.

We had coke boilers at first. The fuel was delivered by train. Just before the bridge over the railway, we had a turntable. The coke truck was shunted off under the College drive where the main boiler was. Then we changed to gas-fired boilers, and later to oil-fired boilers.

That little rail track was built originally for delivering the salt from Droitwich for the medical baths in the old hotel.

The luggage of passengers arriving by train and destined for the hotel (and College) came via the tunnel. It is still there and was always known as The Worm. At the end of term, the girls' trunks stayed in The Worm until the next morning. You couldn't do that today. Then they were loaded onto the trains. Later, we used British Road Services. Now, the girls are collected by their parents in cars, or the girls from abroad go by coach direct to an airport.

The tunnel had an offshoot that was the Icehouse for the Imperial Hotel. Once a year, a history master from Birmingham used to bring his pupils by train to Great Malvern station and take them through The Worm, by our permission. He wanted to show them an actual Victorian station."

Reg Green was a milkman in the 1920's. He recalled, "I had to deliver milk to Malvern Girls' College and most of their boarding houses. When I first began this job, the Misses

Poulton and Greenslade were still in charge and ran the school very efficiently.

Over the years, I must have carried thousands of gallons of milk into that Main Building—the old hotel. It all had to be carried in chums down the back stairs and trundled along various passages into the cold room attached to the kitchen. You never knew in advance how much the College would require. If it was 'milk pudding day', they required many more extra gallons of milk—and it **had** to be found for them.

At one time, my mother was Cook in charge of catering at Malvern Girls' College. My father was night-watchman there too. But they saw very little of each other apart from passing each other in the Guarlford Road near where they lived, as they walked to and from work. During the night, my father used to clean all the girls' shoes—something that is not done now!"

Weather extremes affected a Houseman's work greatly. "In school holidays, when the boarding houses and classrooms were closed, we would find burst pipes in winter," Ken Lynes recalled. "In the bad winter of 1982, I remember seven Housemen hacking away at the ice from the forecourt of Main Building. We had to use pickaxes to get at that ice. It was under a layer of snow. A very hard job, that!

One day, I had a frightening experience, that was nothing to do with the weather. A photographer came to take photos of the Edinburgh Dome, our Sports Hall, close to the College. He wanted to take photos from a great height so, we had to go into Christchurch, next door to the Main Building. I had to accompany this chap up the church steeple.

It was the most frightening job I ever had. We went up a vertical ladder. At the top, you opened a trap door. You caught hold of an old rope, to bend yourself up and over onto the platform. The photographer took photos through the little slits in the steeple.

Coming back, backwards, was frightening. Trying to find the ladder underneath to put your feet on! And carrying his equipment as well—and all in the dark! But he got his photos. *And* I got his priceless equipment down safely."

Old and valuable furniture, left over from the Imperial Hotel days has long been in use in the College, as Ken Lynes testified. "This chaise longue was in the front hall. It was covered all over. Mrs. Gibbs saw the legs at the bottom and said to me. 'I feel that sofa is an antique. Take it into your workshop and strip it down very carefully.' I did. The wood underneath was very ornate. So, it was sent away and returned, restored.

There was only one other clock like our very large and old one. And that one was in the Houses of Parliament. Our clock fetched a tidy sum at the auction in aid of Malvern Priory some years ago."

Epilogue

When a new fire alarm system was being installed in Malvern Girls' College, Ken Lynes rescued three redundant brass fire bells and scraped off their old red paint. Now they gleam as good as new in his own fireplace. Ken cherishes this souvenir of his busy years at the College full of variety and interest—and sheer hard work!

ST. JAMES'S SCHOOL ~ WEST MALVERN

The school was founded in West Malvern by Miss Alice Baird

in 1902 on a beautiful site. Here is Lucy Harris, Head Parlour-maid there in 1904, describing her first sight of St. James's in the book of memories, *"I Was There"*.

"There were tall, stately trees and spring flowers in the coppice. Birds were singing and there was a very happy feeling of restfulness. The house looked majestic with frilled curtains of white muslin in each window.

Inside, the beautiful oak staircase with its brass rods on each step led up to the Music Room. A scotch terrier lay asleep in its basket in the kitchen. There was also an autocratic cat, Kubelik, that wandered about the house.

We, the household staff, were allowed to be present at all forms of entertainment, alongside the ladies of the school. At the Saturday evening dances, when the young ladies wore long white evening dresses, a Scottish gardener played the bagpipes. Oh, the ecstasy of those Saturday evenings!"

Old Girls returning to St. James's many years later, exclaimed, "It was Lucy Harris's pride to remember not only our faces, but also our married names!"

An Old Girl commented, "We received an education based on a code of manners instilled into every girl aided by the inspiring situation of the school with its wonderful view. We looked on the rolling Herefordshire valleys and the blue hills of Wales. There were long hot Sundays in the green shade of the lovely garden, and star-lit walks on winter evenings round the North Hill to study the frosty sky."

Old Girls speak with admiration of Miss Alice Baird, their Headmistress. "Her feelings for beauty, tempered by some Scottish puritanism permeated the school. Her sister, Miss Diana Baird, showed us the beauty of nature as we walked in the woods. She took us blackberrying on wonderful afternoons in the Mathon woods. She read to us and told us delightful stories of her own childhood. Both the Miss Bairds instilled in us a sense of **duty.**"

The British Empire of the early 20th century owed much to the education of St. James's young ladies. "Such girls as did not marry Dukes, probably married outposts of the British Empire."

Miss Alice Baird was Headmistress of St. James's in West Malvern from 1902 until 1948. She left an indelible impression on the school which she had founded.

Another Alice who brought honour to the school was a former pupil, Lady Alice Montagu-Douglas-Scott, who became the Duchess of Gloucester when she married the third son of King George V. Years later, the Duchess sent a photo of herself and her two young sons to St. James's. She had written across it: "Sorry no daughters to follow me at St. James's. Yours, Alice."

Mademoiselle Eva Delpierre taught French at St. James's for 26 years. She was known as "Maddle" and was "small, dynamic and rather fierce". With this gifted teacher, the school won several years running the 'Vase de Sèvres', presented by the President of the French Republic.

A French teacher in Paris said of a former St. James's pupil: "She already spoke good French when she arrived here because she was at the St. James."

Another respected teacher was Fraülein Fodslette who taught German. Her English was fluent but slightly unorthodox. Exasperated with one pupil, she said once, "You are a horse! No. A horse is a **noble** animal. You are a hen!"

Miss Price, who was teaching Dancing and Deportment in 1902, was remembered by generations of St. James's pupils. Her teaching was founded on the Minuet and Court Curtsey.

Miss Price had been trained by a descendant of Mme. d'Egville Michau, a former Mistress of Ceremonies at the Court of George IV.

Old Girls recalled: "Miss Price was petite and most elegant. She would sweep into the room like a queen with a rustle of silk petticoats. Immediately, our backs were straightened, heads went up, and we tried to stand like guardsmen on parade."

A pupil of 1909 remembers: "Miss Price wore a gown the colour of ripe bananas, with her hair curled all over her head. She would be sitting at her piano to teach us dancing and deportment, ready for the Coming-out Ball and the Court curtsey. But in five years' time, the world was at war and all these dandelion clocks were blown away".

Nevertheless, at St. James's, "dances from the Elizabethan Pavane to the late Victorian Gavotte with their colour and grouping made an unforgettable picture against the stone background of the Old Cloisters."

"The Cloisters at St. James's play an important part. They are shelter on stormy days, coolness on hot summer afternoons, and the scene of bazaars and plays. A stone staircase led to the upper cloister. What could have been better for the balcony scene of Romeo and Juliet?"

Miss Rena Cocks taught Music and Drama from 1928 to 1945. She recalled producing a medieval play. "We made clouds of net behind which were to sit Our Lady, St. Nicholas, and St. Gabriel. We hoped these figures would be seen when meant to be seen and hidden when the lights were off. Our indispensable, skilled carpenters, Hill and Wall, made the rock for the Devil, the gate of the monastery and the tower for St. Bernard. And how grateful we were to my landlady, Mrs. Griffith, of West

Malvern for lending us her electric sewing machine to sew the long, long seams of those medieval garments!"

Another teacher who gave long service at St. James's was Miss Mabel Varley, who taught Art there for 21 years. "She was a genius in all stage matters. In 1938, we had a ballet of bats, moths, beetles etc. What fun Miss Varley had designing their fantastic costumes!"

An Old Girl who was a pupil from 1917 to 1921 remembered: "We had hair-brushing sessions carried out by smiling maids. Little Annie brushed our long hair and mended our clothes in a tiny room at the top of the house. What place or occasion could be cosier for a gossip than that crowded, stuffy place, while Annie plied a rhythmic measure with her hairbrush? —such a Victorian pleasure.

After our long hair was washed, we would run about the garden with flowing manes, like drying mermaids."

Grace Harvey, Senior Matron from 1919 to 1929, had a hair-raising experience. "One summer afternoon without permission two young 'monkeys' cut off their lovely tresses. I was devastated. All I could think of was hair, hair, hair. Yes, Margaret's and Catherine's tresses had vanished. What was I to do? I told Miss Diana Baird that evening of the tragedy. She looked after the younger girls. With a smile and a twinkle in her eye, she set my mind at rest, saying, 'It'll grow back in no time.' She had a wonderful personality, always shedding peace and happiness around her."

"By the mid 1920's more than half the school still had long hair, but the number of "bobbed" and "shingled" heads was growing. Only one girl attempted to have a "perm" during the holidays. But the reactions were so awful that the experiment was never repeated!"

Miss Esther Randle, who taught Science and Botany, was delighted with the environment of West Malvern. "Malvern is a wonderful place for a botanist. I can remember the thrill of finding Herb Paris in the school wood. I had never seen it growing before. It is not very common, but local. Later, on a Guide hike, we were sitting down above the old grass tennis courts, and there on the bank was a Bee Orchid. That, too, was an unforgettable moment for me."

Old Girls reminisced: "Every spring we would go to the Bluebell wood and spend happy hours gathering bunches of flowers. The Field Club had expeditions in the damp woods around Mathon and British Camp, which were treasure troves of Fungi. We returned triumphantly, along dark winter lanes clutching japanned boxes oozing with these trophies."

Here are some vivid memories about school meals. "The food was always so good. Some people had a pot of cream each day. They rationed it out—a little for the coffee, some with marmalade, a little more on vegetables.

But Sunday supper was the most dreary cold meat. One day, a group of us refused to eat it. So, we just sat. Miss Alice, our Headmistress, talked to us of everything except meat, and then fed us on delicious cherries! Still no mention of the meat, but strangely enough no further complaints! That was her clever way. In summer we had strawberries or fresh cherries and cream for breakfast."

When shopping in Malvern on Saturdays (between 1905 and 1911) one girl said, "Pocket money went a long way in those days. As we walked in a crocodile down that long winding hill, we knew we should be able to buy what we wanted at a price we could afford. Then tea at George's (opposite the Foley Arms Hotel) and back over the hill on donkeys."

Other memories come flooding back: "I remember the soapy leathery smell of the Boot-hole; the crumpets toasting for tea in the little Sixth Form Room; and drinking the sparkling Malvern water."

At least one pupil detested hockey. "All the winds of heaven met upon the hockey field. How prickly our blue serge blouses were and how long it took to brush mud off a hockey skirt! How greatly I disliked the game! I was always in the wrong place in the field!"

And this glorious location *was* exposed to winter weather. "The wind made your face ache as you plodded round North Hill."

The Great Frost of January 1940 is graphically described by an Old Girl: "It rained, then froze hard. Many of the huge trees in the garden came crashing to the ground. I shall never forget the strangeness of the noise they made. It was like unearthly pistol shots all through the long, almost arctic night."

Fraülein Lucy Elkan, a native German teacher, was at St. James's at a sensitive time—from 1936 to 1939. She recalled: "On summer evenings in St. James's gardens, world affairs seemed blessedly remote despite the ominous threat of war. I felt an unforgettable peace, gazing at the view and returning renewed and restored for another day's work."

This Fraülein was nicknamed 'Cassandra the prophetess'. This was because she was always prophesying doom. She was very concerned about the increasingly alarming state of Nazi Germany, her homeland, when speaking to her friendly but incredulous English colleagues.

When war *did* come in September 1939, Fire Watching patrols had to be organised. Mary Anstruther writes: "We would dress quickly when the siren blared from the top of the

Mathematics Room. We would patrol the top of the roof or crouch out of the wind behind one of the skylights. We would listen to the steady beat of the German aircraft engines passing overhead. One hour, and back they would come from Birmingham or Coventry. Two or three hours, and we knew the raid had been on Liverpool.

I well remember the night of the great raid on Coventry, and how people went up the hills to see the fire reflected red on the low clouds to the North.

Miss C. Burchardt kept her horse down at Croft Farm. Her duty, on certain nights, was to ride up the Beacon and visit the lookout post there. We never fully understood the objects of these visits. But these starlight rides gave a touch of romance to what was otherwise a cold, boring vigil."

To help the war effort, pupils and staff took on extra duties. There was potato and fruit picking on some afternoons instead of games. Because of a shortage of maids, there were rotas for laying tables, waiting at tables, and washing up. They made camouflage nets. They dried herbs, nettles and rose hips for pharmacies. The girls knitted endless khaki garments, full of dropped stitches.

Miss Anstruther knitted rapidly vast sea boot stockings and immense naval sweaters. Meanwhile, she heard girls in Prep. "recite" their English Literature poetry. She seldom dropped a stitch.

There were paper shortages. The Malvern Gazette was cut down in size in July 1942. Its familiar cover disappeared until December 1945 when the war had ended.

A former St. James's pupil wrote this thoughtful comment about the war. "We realised, when the war in Europe ended, how much difference the *little* annoyances of war had made in our daily life.

The air raid siren would no longer have its practice in the middle of an elocution lesson. There would be no further need for blackout. The dusty sandbags would be taken away from the tunnel.

The news of the victory was given out at supper. I remember earlybedders hunting enthusiastically for red, white, and blue socks, to hang out of the windows. Next morning, the first thing I saw was Miss Anstruther scaling the front gates to hang out a flag in celebration.

The Beacon again fulfilled its old purpose, with a bonfire on the summit, which passed on the joyful news to Hereford and on into Wales."

Another Old Girl recorded her happy memories of the non-academic people who help a school to keep going in wartime. "There was Mr. Tyte the hairdresser. Week after week he washed our hair with his own particular brand of strongly scented, bright green shampoo. There were the carpenters and groundsmen, Pitt and Hammond, and the taxi driver, Mr. Bennett, from the garage in the village.

There was something reliable and unchanging about them all. How much we appreciated that, amidst all the turbulence of growing up, combined with the insecurity created by the war. People mattered tremendously to us, then."

LAWNSIDE

The school was founded in about 1857 in Elmsdale, Abbey Road, Malvern, by Miss Caroline Cooper. Lawnside joined St. James and the Abbey in 1994.

Miss Winifred Barrows was Headmistress at Lawnside for 35 years—from 1925 to 1960. She seems to have been a very democratic Headmistress, with a warm personality, wide interests, resourceful, and open to fresh ideas.

She offered Lawnside and its gardens in Albert Road South as a venue for social occasions during the Malvern Festivals in the 1930's. Sir Edward Elgar and Dame Laura Knight, the artist, were friends of Miss Barrows.

We learn much of interest about Lawnside from the history of the school, compiled by Mary Dixey and Duseline Stewart. "The outstanding event of the week, in the Festival of 1929, was the Lawnside garden party given by Sir Barry Jackson. Here, on the beautiful lawns assembled three hundred and forty guests. It was the hottest day of the year, but the fine trees provided a welcome shade. Many pretty summery dresses were worn, but I'm afraid I had eyes only for Ernest Thesiger's lemon tie and Bernard Shaw's mauve stockings."

Disney Reynolds remembered Miss Barrows: "I worked for many years at the high-class grocer's in Great Malvern—Tipping and Morris. Lawnside in those days of the 1930's was THE school. If the girls did well, Miss Barrows would think nothing of coming up to the shop and ordering 30 boxes of chocolates. Nothing was spared. Miss Barrows was one of the leading lights of Malvern Festival and Sir Barry Jackson was one of the big noises."

In contrast to the grandeur of garden parties, "whcn Miss Barrows went up into the town with her old-fashioned bicycle (she never learned to drive) she wore a small 'halo' hat on the back of her head. The Queen wore a similar hat, then in fashion.

As she freewheeled back down the hill, she would clasp

her hat with one hand and the brakes with the other, while her shopping bags hung precariously from the handlebars."

Old Girls of Lawnside recall their schooldays nostalgically: "As it was a lovely moonlight night, Miss Barrows decided to take us all for a walk on the hills. So, in our long 'crocodile' we followed her up the Happy Valley and round by St. Ann's Well."

Miss Barrows endeared herself to her pupils by her impromptu and somewhat unorthodox decisions. "Whole holidays were magic", said one Old Girl. "We would pick wild daffodils and walk over the hills from the Beacon to British Camp to a supper of egg and chips. Then home by bus. We spent Midsummer Eve at the top of Midsummer Hill, where we entertained each other, and back to school after midnight."

I like the description of the school uniform before 1920. "Our tunics were brown, as were our blazers and long winter coats. It was a lovely light 'goldy' brown. The Sunday hats were very pretty. They were of a very fine soft straw, brown on top and a soft pink underneath the brim, and one pink rose on the side of the brim."

One of Lawnside's young ladies recollects: "Once, I started driving off the first tee of a well-known golf club. My ball went straight down the fairway, but not very far. A man standing by remarked, "A very nice ladylike drive!" "Yes," I retorted, "I was educated at a very ladylike school!"

Memories of schooldays during the Second World War are interesting. "Some of the girls did 'war work' by gathering herbs, foxglove leaves and nettles, to be dried and sent off to a firm of London druggists. Elgar's daughter, Mrs. Elgar Blake, was the County representative of the Women's Institute for herb collecting. She gave a talk at Lawnside and advised on the best methods of drying what had been collected."

"Food in wartime was not easy, but the Lawnside cook did wonders. Even the occasional carrot-on-toast at breakfast tasted far better than it sounds. Jam, honey, marmalade could only be one pound jar per month, per person. Later, it was a mere half pound. But at tea-time, other delicacies appeared— 'Yeastrel', 'Betrox' and a fearsome brown concoction which proclaimed itself to be 'chocolate spread'."

"In 1944, King George VI and Queen Elizabeth came to Malvern to visit the Radar Establishment, which had taken over Malvern College for the war years.

Miss Barrows took the school along to line the route in College Road. An Old Girl remembers being instructed to 'step forward and curtsey' as the Royal car drove past. But this was forgotten when the great moment came, and they—like everyone else—just waved and cheered."

Mary Dixey, a pupil at Lawnside in wartime, remembers: "Several times during our morning break, we saw cascades of silver paper strips fluttering down from the sky. We often gathered up handfuls of them.

We had no idea that the Radar Establishment, which had come to Malvern in the war, had been using these strips to test radar screens in rehearsals for the D-Day invasion."

Let us conclude with happy memories of the Coronation Day of the present Queen Elizabeth II on 2nd June 1953. A Lawnside girl recalled: "We had a special Coronation dinner at school:

> Hors d'oeuvre—Crown Jewels grapefruit
> Poulet Froid Couronnement
> Jambon Westminster
> Salade Buckingham Palace

Melba Windsor Castle

To 'crown' everything, we were given a beautiful cake in the shape of a crown from the Dorothy Café in Church Street. This cake had decorated the shop window for two days. We felt it was a great honour to have it for our own dining room. Miss Schneider, the proprietress, is always so kind to us."

This was surely an appropriate gesture by the Dorothy Café. By 1953, generations of Lawnside girls had been customers at the confectioners' shops in Malvern for the past one hundred years!

THE ABBEY SCHOOL MALVERN WELLS

Because she lived in Malvern Wells, as a child, Joy Van Daesdonk had vivid memories of the Abbey School there. "I remember that the school was founded in Victorian times by Miss Alice and Miss Florence Judson. They owned all the big houses as well, and they were used for boarding houses for the girls.

My grandfather came up to Malvern from Devon. Eventually, he became Head Gardener at the Abbey School. They had vast gardens and the vegetable gardens fed the pupils there. At that school, there were two chauffeurs because they had two cars of their own at the Abbey.

The girls were not allowed to go on the bus. If they went out, they always had a teacher with them. This was in the 1930's up until the war. If the girls went any distance, they were chauffeur driven. The chauffeurs had a blue uniform and black gaiters. The girls' uniform was grey with red and white. They wore boaters and used to walk in crocodiles.

I entered the Abbey School on one memorable occasion. For our School Certificate exams, we had to go to a Centre, as our private school in Malvern Link was too small. And the Centre where I had to take my exams was at the Abbey School! I thought that going inside there would be very 'upper crust'.

But I was disillusioned. We had a whole morning of exams with a break in the middle. I went to where the Abbey girls had their elevenses. You could have milk or cocoa. I think I thought I was going to be offered caviar!

To my surprise, I was presented with a large crust of bread and dripping! 'If this is the Abbey School boarding school life?!' I thought. It seemed to be very austere—nothing luxurious."

Wedding photo of Alice Davies and Reginald Betteridge c.1910. Alice Betteridge was the third generation to run donkeys on Malvern Hills. Reginald Betteridge was a small farmer, well known as a Trainer of both horses and recruits in the Worcestershire Yeomanry.

Donkey boys on Malvern Hills c. 1910.

Alice Betteridge with donkey riders c. 1910. The smiling girl, far right, is Winifred Barrows, who was later to become Headmistress of Lawnside School, Malvern.

Donkey riders in the 1940's. Alice Betteridge stands far right.

The Davis family from Upper Welland picnic with friends on Malvern Hills in the 1930's.

Pupils of Malvern Wells Junior and Infants School c.1900.

Pupils of Malvern Wells Junior and Infants School c.1910.

*Six-year-old pupils of Pickersleigh Road Council School,
Malvern in 1931. Dennis Morgan, wearing braces, and
looking puzzled, is seated in the middle of the second row.*

*Minna Bowers with her 1962 class at
Cromwell Road C. of E. Primary School.*

West Malvern C. of E. School present gifts to Mary Tudge in 1981. Mary had been involved with the school for 33 years, as parent of four sons, lunchtime supervisor and clerical ancillary. Photo courtesy Malvern Gazette & Ledbury Reporter.

The Duke of Edinburgh opens the Edinburgh Dome Sports Hall, Malvern Girls' College, on 4th May 1978. Behind him is (left) Professor Bryan Brooke, Admiral Rodney Sturdee (Bursar) and Headmistress, Miss Veronica Owen. Photo courtesy Malvern Gazette & Ledbury Reporter.

In the 1950's, Malvern College Prefects were still wearing boaters and carrying silver-topped canSces.

Exiled to Blenheim Palace in the 1939-45 war, Malvern College's School House were offered the Long Library as their dormitory. Note the coconut matting on the parquet floors and the statues cloaked in blankets.

Staff at The Chase Forge, Barnards Green, c.1900. The owner, WM. Reynolds, stands in front, wearing a bowler hat.

This early 1900's photo shows Mr. Alfred Davis, upholsterer, and his son, Edward, in their roomy workshop, which still stands today in the garden of his house in Sandford, Upper Welland, now occupied by his daughter, Margaret Davis.

Malvern Common Laundry, 54 Longridge Road, Poolbrook, c.1905.
Mr. A. Bird, Proprietor, is surrounded by his staff.

Sam Bird and Walter Little, apple picking at Clevelode in 1959.

James Carty at work for Malvern District Council in Malvern in the 1920's.

Eliza Carty with four of her seven children.

James Carty and three friends, c.1910

James Carty and the same three friends in battle dress c.1914

Five of the young Cartys.

This photo, taken on Malvern Hills in 1935, shows two of the Carty sons with their local friends. Pictured from left are Gerald Carty, E. Evans, J. McCary, G. Heath, Dick Carty, Arthur Brown, A. Finch, A. Lowe, G. Lewis, R. Lewis.

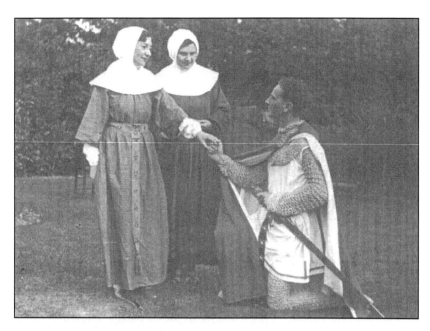

In July 1938, St. Matthias Dramatic Society presented an episode of Ledbury history, entitled "Katharine Audley". Here, Katharine, (Gwen Forster) offers her hand to a knight. Minna Bowers stands behind.

These 'Victorian ladies' appeared in a large and significant historical pageant in 1947. The pageant took place in the old Vicarage Garden of St. Matthias-at-the-Link. Gwen Forster, who was Wardrobe Mistress, stands in the centre.

Rogation-tide procession through a cherry orchard, to Triggs Farm in Yates Hay Road, arrives to bless the crops—an old tradition of the Church.

The blessing of crops and farm animals at Triggs Farm, Yates Hay Road, Malvern Link.

Snow White and the Seven Dwarfs was performed by children of St. Matthias' church. Madge Howard Davies produced this pantomime in 1948. Photo courtesy Malvern Gazette & Ledbury Reporter.

May Queen (Paddy Spencer) right, meets Forget-me-not Queen (Elizabeth Hartley), with their attendants, in the grounds of St. Matthias church.

Brian Beale, aged 8, wearing the uniform of a pupil of the Lyttelton Grammar School and a chorister at Malvern Priory in 1921.

Malvern Link Men's Own Brotherhood 25th Anniversary 1908-1933. James Carty, from Barbados, is in second row from back. Clem Walton, photographer, sits sideways in the front row. He not only took the photo but played the violin!

Canon John Davies crowns May Queen, Sarah Pemble, c.1981.
Photo courtesy Norman May's Studio, Worcester.

Canon John Davies presents the crozier to Boy Bishop, Lee Baker.
Photo courtesy Norman May's Studio, Worcester.

*The May Queen and Boy Bishop ceremony inside St. Matthias church
c.1980. Canon John Davies stands behind, in the centre.
Photo courtesy Norman May's Studio, Worcester.*

Cridlan & Walker, the oldest shop in Malvern, was established in 1830. This photo was taken in 1906.

Advertisement in "Handbook of Malvern" dated 1858. This warehouse was the forerunner of Tipping and Morris, High Class Grocers.

Lady's fashion of 1903, on sale at Cox and Painter's department store, named Warwick House, after the first proprietor.

BRAYS OF MALVERN

1895 – 1995
CELEBRATING 100 YEARS

Brays of Malvern façade at the turn of the century, early 1900's.

Burley's Hairdressing Salon-cum-Tobacconist's, established in 1920. Mr. Harry Burley and his son, Dennis, stand together in the middle with their staff.

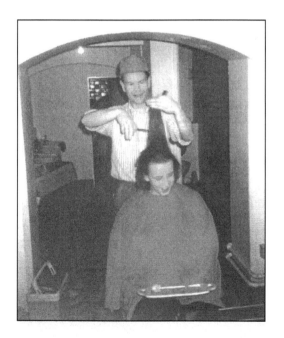

David Burley, ever cheerful, carries on his family hair-dressing business in the third generation. His customer here is Dave Powis of Malvern College, where long hair is banned.

The Queen Mother attended celebrations for the Centenary of Malvern College in 1965. Here she is shaking hands with Wilfred Hoskins, staff instructor for the College's Army Cadet Force, which had formed a Royal Guard of Honour.

The Queen Mother talks with John Tompkins, Chairman of Malvern Urban District Council, at the Centenary of Malvern College, in 1965. Mr. Donald Lindsay, Headmaster, stands on left.

A Coronation Parade in 1937, when King George VI was crowned. The parade marched from Upper Welland to Wells House Playing Fields in Woodfarm Road, Malvern Wells.

A street party to celebrate VE Day 1945, at the end of World War II. This party took place in Pound Bank Road, Barnards Green.

10 ~ We Earned Our Living

. . . .

CHIMNEY SWEEP

"My father, Samuel Bird, was a chimney sweep", said Francis Bird. "He began chimney sweeping in the 1920's until the late 1950's. I can remember him in 1930. He had an old-fashioned shop bike with a frame on the front, where he put his brushes, his soot bag, and his sheet for the fireplace. Then there was his brush and shovel to clean up the soot afterwards. And his rods were alongside the bar of his bike. He never owned a car.

He travelled to Upton, Callow End, out to Welland, the Hanleys, Colwall, West Malvern and Malvern Link. He would sweep a chimney for one shilling and sixpence.

Samuel Bird didn't carry the soot around with him. He had various places where he could leave it. Three or four times a year, we went up to my uncle's laundry in Longridge Road to borrow his horse and cart, to collect in all the soot.

Father had allotments like all the villagers behind the Foley Institute. We put the soot in a shed there. Everybody came to buy a bag of soot for sixpence, to put on the garden. They all said soot was a good thing to lighten the ground. It also stopped the slugs.

My father swept chimneys at Malvern College, Malvern

Girls' College, and the Abbey Hotel. He was one of the very few chimney sweepers in the district."

Samuel Bird's old bike was renovated by his grandson. His son, Francis, recently had a letter from a Leicester man, who has bought this old Raleigh bike for £100 at a Vintage sale. He now displays it at Vintage rallies!

MARKET GARDENER

Austin Hartwright recalled, "In 1917, my father was a market gardener at The Hook near Welland. He had always got a job for us boys at home—washing onions or radishes or lettuce, ready for the next day. Or we had to pick fruit—blackcurrants, plums, apples, pears. When we had picked gooseberries, we had to 'stalk and eye' them.

We sold fruit to the hotels in Malvern—The Abbey and the Foley Arms. When we had picked a big hamper of 80 pounds' weight, we boys could go out to play.

The Malvern market was on every Saturday in a big market hall at the bottom of Edith Walk. On that day, father used to ride his bicycle into Malvern, leaving me, aged 13, and my younger brother to bring the produce to sell. We used to pack a big old-fashioned twins' pram with our greenstuff. There was a sack of potatoes underneath on the springs, and rhubarb tied on top.

At 7 a.m. we two boys pushed that heavy pram up into Malvern and got to the market at 9 a.m. One of us pulled it with a cord at the front, and the other pushed from behind.

When we reached Malvern, we used to have to take a basket each and sell the stuff round the houses in Graham Road and so on. For lunch, Dad sent us to the Gateway butcher. For three pence we got pieces of steak, liver, etc. We used to cook them over a gas stove and have our meal there in the market.

Coming home at night with the pram empty, my brother used to get in the pram, and I used to stand on the back, and away we'd ride down the hills to home. *That* was quite easy-going. It was fun!"

OSTLER

"My father was an ostler," said Disney Reynolds. "He was born in about 1860 and he worked for Cridlan and Walker at the Abbey Gateway. Every morning, he turned out six floats with their horses for the shop. He kept all the harnesses and turned out the ponies.

He started his work early morning and they finished early at night. They had a big staff. Father had to go round with the Head Shopman. He wore a white smock and a white apron. They took meat round to the hotels and all the Colleges.

Unfortunately, like a good many more, he was very fond of beer. Mother had to suffer for it. But he lived till he was about 78. He was still on his feet for his Golden Wedding. Then he died of cancer. He did quite well considering the life he led!"

SADDLER

Disney Reynolds recalled, "In the 1920's, in the corner of Newtown Road, there was an old-fashioned saddler's—a man named Barrow. He was the master man. The Lady Beauchamp of those days used to drive up from Madresfield Court, in her landau with the coachman, and bring the harness to be mended. I always remember seeing him come out, bowing to Her Ladyship."

FARMING IN THE 1890's

Ethel Hall, aged 107, recalled, "I was born on 7th December 1890, on a farm in Mere, Somerset. My father used to send some cows to market at Wells and Glastonbury. This was in the days when cattle were driven on foot to London. They had to stop en route to be shod like horses so that their hooves did not wear out."

FARMING IN THE EARLY 1900's

Bill Sims was born in 1906 at Paddock Cottage, Clevelode Lane. His father, William, worked at Home Farm, Madresfield, then known as Penn Farm. There, he looked after the magnificent grey Shire horses which worked on the land. They were entered for ploughing contests. At least 12 men worked there at that time. Bill remembers the blacksmiths on the farm, the cowman, the hurdle maker, the gamekeeper, and the dairymaids.

Bill took the morning's milk from Clevelode Farm to the railway station in Malvern by horse and cart. It travelled by train to Birmingham. In good weather, the milk went daily to the Open Air School in West Malvern. This was a tuberculosis hospital. The milk from Clevelode Farm was classified Grade A, which meant it was tuberculosis free.

WORKING WITH HORSES

Donald Treherne told me, "I worked for Dipple, Coal

Merchants. I delivered coal, or blocks of wood, twice a day to Hanley Swan or to West Malvern. It was hard work for our carthorses. And I was a tree surgeon too.

My favourite horse, a grey, was Dinah. Horses know if you like them or not. Some horses were kickers or biters. I bought brass martingales for them to wear on their harness."

LAUNDRY WORKERS

Francis Bird related: "There were a lot of laundries on the commons. Mrs. Cotterell, on the north side of Geraldine Road, had a laundry on the Poolbrook common. She used to do the laundry for the Colleges and some of the hotels. She did it all by hand, squeezed it through her mangle, and put it on lines on the common. Nothing ever got stolen.

For line posts, they used to get a railway sleeper and split it through the middle and put them in the ground. She would iron her laundry in her kitchen. I can see her now. Flat irons on hobs by the coal fire. Electric irons had not been invented!

Further up the village of Poolbrook was another laundry doing the same thing. That was Granny Brookes. You could hear the wind on the common going through the sheets, flapping them. The pegs then were wooden, made by the old gypsies. They would come round selling them—made of ash branch, split down, and bound with tin.

My uncle's laundry on the common was the major laundry. They worked for the very big Colleges, the Abbey Hotel, and the Tudor Hotel. My uncle had a horse and dray to transport his laundry. He was Albert Bird. He had a staff of 10 or 12 girls.

Although it was a golf course, where the washing hung to

dry, the golfers didn't use that area. But the sheep and the cows roaming on the common, would go **underneath** the sheets. We used to call the sheep and cows "the 500 green-keepers". They belonged to the householders who owned ground adjacent to the common … the people who had Commoners' Rights."

'Divvy' Davis agreed: "Washing lines were fixtures on the Wyche common. On Mondays, they were laden with white sheets. Some of the mothers washed for the gentry in Peach-field Road. One house I knew there had 23 servants including gardeners and grooms—looking after just 5 residents!"

Doris Smith, who lived with her parents at Aldwyn Tower Hotel, said: "Our washerwoman was Mrs. Haines. She was a big woman. I made a dress for her once. I couldn't get the tape measure round her hips without her holding it on. She had a very strong Worcestershire accent. She loved coming to us. She had 10 children in a very small cottage in West Malvern. Her husband had an allotment to feed them all. She walked over the hill to us and brought us something from her allotment.

Our housemaids would sit her down to peel shallots, which she did very well, and with never a tear in her eyes! Then they gave her the remains of the big rice pudding to eat in the kitchen. Later on, she came to us by what she called the BUZZ."

BAKER AND CONFECTIONER

"I was apprenticed to the baking trade," said Austin Hart-wright. "I worked in the bakehouse of George's Restaurant—a big shop opposite the Foley Arms in Great Malvern.

It was hard work. The bread dough had to be made by hand. Cakes? We made cream horns, puff pastry, éclairs. All through the summer we made our own ice creams. They were flavoured with real strawberries and real cream. You had to turn the machine by hand to freeze the mixture. Vanilla ices were made with real eggs, milk, and vanilla sticks.

George's was the biggest restaurant in town apart from the hotels. On Open Days all the Colleges' parents came down to us. In a room apart, they enjoyed their iced drinks and ice creams.

At the end of the First World War, everybody was having parties. A tremendous amount of coach trips came from Wales to Malvern. We were real busy … packed out day after day all through the summer of 1919. I had to carve the meat for 130 people at a time. By then I was working in the restaurant.

Then I worked for Lewis's bakery for 32 years. When I retired, they presented me with a gold watch, inscribed with my name and the date—1965."

THE HOTEL 'BOOTS'

Before the First World War, Disney Reynolds remembered the man who cleaned the boots for residents of the Imperial Hotel (now the Malvern Girls' College). "He was a man named Dance, who lived up North Malvern Road. He was a well-known billiard player, and he could also mend clocks."

DOMESTIC SERVICE

Lady Emily Foley, who was the Lady of the Manor of Malvern, in Victorian times, lived at Stoke Edith. One of the villagers there remembered that Lady Foley gave the local schoolgirls red and black capes. Red was her livery colour. The girls had to curtsey to her.

Mrs. Hatfield, who was a child in the village of Stoke Edith in the 1920's, used to admire the black satin dress and lace cap of a woman who was in service at the big house of Lady Foley's. The little girl wanted to go into service too!

Her own mother had been in service to a lady in Hereford. Her mother said she had to wear a chamois leather apron under her coat. The apron had pockets to hold her lady's jewels!

Dorothy Pembridge's mother was Head Nurse to the Lygon family at Madresfield Court from 1906. She told Dorothy, "Christmas was a lovely time at the Court. There were so many guests, Staff Balls, and suppers, that the housemaids did not get to bed. They changed into their print dresses and scraped the candle-fat off the polished floors, dropped from the candelabras."

IN SERVICE AT MADRESFIELD COURT

Rose Nash told me: "I came to Madresfield Court in 1935. I was housemaid. There were 5 other housemaids then, one cook, a kitchen maid, and a scullery maid. My future mother-in-law worked in the kitchen, plucking all the poultry. She lived at the Lodge. I used to go down there on my half-days. There I met Harold, her son. We started going out together.

All the housemaids used the Donkey on the staircase and front hall. It was a flat piece of iron with a broom handle. We had to put old blankets underneath it and push to polish. That was after you'd put the beeswax and turpentine on the floor. We had to make our own polish! And you got down on your knees to put the polish on.

My mother used to wear those fleecy-lined knickers. I used to get all her old ones—they were pinks and blues—and take them back to use on the Donkey. No Hoovers then! We had to use dustpan and brush in the 1930's. The dust was flying about. No wonder I had bronchitis. I've always had that.

When I went back there in 1953, we were up about 6.30 a.m. and back on duty again for the evenings when we had to turn the beds down and take up hot water in cans. There was no hot water in the bedrooms then. While they were at dinner, we had to tidy the Drawing Room and empty the ashtrays. We lived in and had our meals in the Servants' Hall.

The first day I went back there, Miss Hook was Head Housemaid. She was tall. She had on her black dress, and lace on top of her head. 'Go to your room and change into your black dress,' she said to me. 'Then come down to tea in the Housemaids' Sitting Room.' I did. I remember seeing for tea some thick bread and marge and a 2-pound jam pot on the table. And the bed was hard! I cried that night. All those stiff dresses we had to wear!

We had to clean the grates of steel and the brass pokers and tongs for the open fires. We had quite decent food. On Sundays, we had a little service in the Court Chapel, by the local Vicar."

QUARRYMEN AND BRICK WORKERS

Joy Van Daesdonk recalled: "There were still a lot of quarrymen about in the early 1930's. Some lived down Upper Welland Road. We saw them pushing their bicycles up our hill on their way to work. And people used to walk miles to get to work then." The last quarry ceased to work about 25 years ago.

"I used to see an elderly couple who worked in the North Malvern brickworks. And they looked so tired and so dirty with the brick dust. You'd think they worked in a coal mine. You used to see people then who looked as if they had worked hard." At North Malvern quarry, they blew a whistle at 12 noon and 4 p.m. to warn about the blasting.

BANK CLERK

"I was the first woman bank clerk in the Midland Bank in Worcester," declared Elizabeth Guise Berrow. She was 104 years old when she told me: "This would be in about 1914. I had taken lessons in shorthand and typewriting. The men were being called up into the army when I entered the bank. They were desperately in need of someone. I was interviewed. The Bank Manager had already interviewed my Headmistress at the Girls' Grammar School in Worcester. He said to me, 'Can you start next week? Can you come on Thursday?' I did. I stayed there 30 years in the same branch."

CARPENTER AND CABINET MAKER

"I was an apprentice carpenter, working for Broads in Broads Bank, Great Malvern," said Reginald Hall-Robinson.

I had to do a lot of sandpapering and moulding. The machines weren't so perfect then. I had to put the shavings in a dust sheet and carry them over my shoulder, and down Broads Bank to Victoria Road, where there was an allotment belonging to Broads. That's where I put the shavings. In the corner of this yard, was a blacksmith's shop. Aye, Mr. Jeynes.

I used to watch him smacking the iron about.

Broads done all the woodwork in all the banks in Malvern.

In the Midland Bank at the top of Church Street the wood-work is walnut.

I used to find great pleasure in working in wood because it always seemed to be *alive*. Mahogany always seems so *warm* to me. Aye, oak's nice but I'd rather have mahogany, myself. Of course, it isn't used a lot, like oak is, in beams and buildings. But mahogany *do* look warm, don't it, like?

Nowadays they talk about pine. One time it all come from Russia, I think. Now you gets pine, and the more knots in it, the more they likes it!"

At the age of 92, Reginald proudly showed me some of his creations: a doll's house, a roll top desk, a miniature windmill in the garden, a spinning wheel in the conservatory, a mahogany cabinet.

"And I've made about 50 corner cupboards since I retired aged 70", added Reginald. He is a true craftsman—a rare discovery.

BUILDING A HOUSE

"I built this bungalow two years after the war," said 'Divvy' Davis. "I was trained in the building trade, properly. That wall—my wife, 'er, put all them stones in that. *She* done it. The house cost just over £1,000 in materials. I made all the floors, doors, windows, and roof.

But of course, if you've trained properly, it makes such a difference. So many men—they knows a certain amount about making windows—but that's finished them! They can't do anything else!"

WORKING ON THE RAILWAY

In the days of steam engines, when the pace of life was so much slower, to be a railwayman had a status value. It was considered a job for life. Great pride was taken in one's work.

The Station Master was much respected. He wore uniform and a top hat and lived in a house on the station. Awards were won for the best kept stations with the brightest flower beds and the name picked out in white pebbles. Trains were important in transporting agricultural products to market. Pigeons in baskets were released by railwaymen at times prescribed.

The signalmen had quite a lonely job if they were in a remote area. But they had the radio to keep them awake. And in their spare time, they mended clocks or grew tomatoes.

Donald Treherne remarked: "My father was a signalman. He had an allotment near the signal box. As there weren't many trains on that line, he could tend his vegetables between times."

Gary Taylor said: "I started to work here on Malvern Link station on 25th February 1974. When I retire, that will make 50 years altogether for me on the railway. I've enjoyed it very much, but I've seen quite a few changes. I've seen all the steam engines go out. They didn't knock this Link station down until 1971–72."

Frank Bowers told me: "I worked on the railway for 42 years. I started as a lad porter, aged 16, at Malvern Link Goods, and finished as a Movements Inspector at Birmingham. As a lad porter, I was expected to have the fires lit when the clerks came on duty at 7 o'clock. I finished after 4 o'clock, when the boss had finished signing the letters.

My main duty was to work the weighbridge. There were

two. One was a truck weighbridge. There were up to 60 truck-loads of Malvern stone from the quarries per day. And there were several coal merchants operating in the area also.

In 1934, Malvern Link Goods station was extremely busy, dealing with freight trains bringing all kinds of food. Every morning we had a truck bringing meat from Smithfield market in London. A driver delivered sides of beef from London to local butchers. Fish would arrive all through the day and was collected by local fishmongers. Milk in churns was collected by trains on branch lines.

There were wagons of fruit in summer. We started off with the pea season—truckloads of peas from local growers to be sent to markets in big cities all over the country. There would be cherries from the Teme Valley; strawberries, plums from Pershore and Evesham, right through until Brussel sprouts in the autumn.

Labels were made out of three categories—for livestock (such as cattle) or fresh meat, for coal or stone, and for goods for the railway's own use. The address and route had to be written with an extra thick pencil. So that a shunter with an oil lamp at night in heavy snow could read what was on the side of the loaded truck. And those wagon loads had to be transferred at various marshalling yards.

But they only gave us half a pencil! That was because the Great Western and the London Midland and Scottish railways shared the stationery and the labour and the profits.

The Great Western was considered the premier line. In the 1920's and 1930's the CHELTENHAM FLYER from London Paddington to Cheltenham was the fastest train in the world. It took one hour."

HOPYARD WORKER

Rose Nash told me: "My father was a wire worker in Hereford-shire hopyards. He built up hopyards and repaired the wires. He would walk miles. He never had a bicycle or a car.

He would start out from home about 4 a.m. on foot. He went to different farms—Pudge's and Lewis's. Other men were working with him. They had a lorry to carry the wire. It was wound on a round barrel."

FIREMAN

"I was 17 when I joined the Fire Brigade in Malvern," said Eric Jones. "Because of my ability to run fast, I was taken on in 1927 as a retained fireman. We used to be called by a steam hooter. It went for two minutes. You dropped everything and got on your bike to get to the fire station. We were in Victoria Road then. We entered national competitions. There were set drills and First Aid and rescuing people.

The hill fires were bad. A lorry coming down British Camp hill set the hills on fire. That fire went to the Wyche Cutting. We were paid four shillings for the turnout and three shillings and sixpence an hour for the first four hours. We got two shillings and sixpence an hour after that. We were well paid! Quite a bit of pocket money at times—especially on the hills!"

LIBRARIAN IN A SHOP

Helen Cutler told me: "I worked first of all in Wood's Royal Library, which was where Barclays Bank is now in Great Malvern at the top of Church Street. That belonged to a Miss Woods. The china shop nearby was her brother's.

Wood's Royal Library was a huge shop. I worked there for a year for nothing, 'cos it was a privilege to be there. They had a big library. And they sold postcards and books and beautiful things like leather goods. My recollection is of beautiful lustre china. It was the fashion in those days.

Then I worked at W.H. Smith's in Malvern Link—which is now Ladbrokes. They had a library and Boots did too. At W.H. Smith's we employed about 10 paperboys. They went to Suckley, Madresfield—everywhere, on their bikes. There was a big trade in newspapers."

GLOVEMAKER

Leslie Lawrence recalled: "My Uncle Harry travelled by bus all the way from Walsall into Worcester, every day, for his job. He was a glovemaker. He used to leave home at 5 a.m. to get to work at 9 a.m. He would leave work at 5 p.m. to reach home at 9 p.m.

We still have one piece of his equipment. It's a ruler 14 inches long. It has 4 sides. It's like a pyramid that's wider at the bottom than at the top. He measured with it and turned the glove inside out. That was his personal 'stick'."

TAILOR

Joan Preece said: "All my dad's brothers were tailors. My Uncle Willy kept this little shop in Old Street, Upton-on-Severn. He done quite a lot of work for the Coventry family. In those days all their riding habits were hand-made. He had to go to Croome Court to measure his clients. He was a very busy man, Uncle Willy.

In Hartlebury Castle Museum I found this sign: WAL-
TON, BREECHES MAKER. That was Uncle Willy. And
there was also a stuffed fox's head there, that he used to have in
his window, and a hunting cap."

TAILORESS

Brenda Lawrence told me: "In the 1950's I was a trainee tai-
loress in London. The first day we were given a pair of scissors
that were one foot long. They had great thick blades. Then they
gave us a load of wadding and big thick pads, 'cos everything
had thick shoulder pads then.

I am still friends to this day with Clare, the other trainee
who started with me. We said, 'A piece of cake!' But by the end
of the day, our hands were black and blue!

With a square piece of chalk, we had to use rulers as long as
your arm to draw lines 6 inches apart. We had to sew with great
big needles, wearing topless thimbles on our middle fingers.
And the material was very thick tweed.

But it couldn't have been so bad, 'cos I was there for 7 years
with my mate. We made costumes (jacket and skirt) and coats.
All my work was done by hand. There were about 100 of us in
one great big room.

After 7 years I went into a West End firm that did bespoke
tailoring. It was piece work there. **They** were slave drivers, and
I missed the company of the other workers.

My first firm preferred girls to boys, 'cos girls were quicker
and had more supple fingers. When they threw down the bales
of wool material on the tables, all the fluff came up and you'd
choke!"

MILLINER

Ivy Dance recalled: "At the age of four, before starting school, I used to visit Florrie, a milliner, in her home. I watched Florrie trim hats for weddings. Sitting on a stool, I learnt to run a needle through a ribbon, to ruche it to form a 'flower'. Thus my interest in millinery was born.

At the age of 16, I began as an apprentice at Gertrude Mitchell's shop in High Street, Worcester. The Head milliner had six girls at her table in the back of the shop. We worked on straw hats in winter months and felt hats in the summer, ready for winter. I was there for 8 years until I married at age 24.

You had to do perfect work to satisfy the Head milliner, and measure the brims, peaks, and crowns accurately. One customer had chosen a grey hat to match her grey suit for a wedding. She requested that her hat be trimmed with mauve 'wisteria'. I had not heard of wisteria. I didn't know what it looked like. But I soon learnt!

Sometimes, felt hats had pokerwork designs on the crown or brim. A tiny 'sparkler-like' poker was held over the gas flame to make accurate holes in the felt.

We made hats only to order—for weddings etc., and only for Harrods and other London firms. Queen Mary was one of our customers."

UPHOLSTERER

"My father, Alfred Davis, was an upholsterer in Upper Welland", said Margaret Davis. "He built his roomy workshop in the garden. Before that, he worked under a large chestnut tree. Among his customers was the Wells House School. He would repair mattresses for this school.

Mostly, he renovated chairs and settees. And they were some wrecks some of them! He used a lot of horsehair in those days. But it became scarce, so he used coconut fibre instead. And he used wool. The last covering was wadding—the real stuff. It stopped the horsehair working through. And there was canvas between the different layers.

He came here to this house in 1908. We were seven children. I was the last one. I was born here and have lived here ever since. My father's workshop is still there in the garden."

HAIRDRESSER AND BARBER

"My grandfather established our Hairdresser's in 1920", said David Burley. "In the early 1930's, he took on the boys of Malvern College. I go there about four evenings a week. In a term, I get through about 1,500 haircuts. Quite a few come from the Far East these days. And there are Germans, Russians ... They talk about their countries. You can learn a lot. It's very interesting.

I remember when I started there back in the '60's, they still had fagging then. The first-year boys had to clean a Prefect's shoes and run errands for him. I saw all this. It was abolished in about 1965. Under Mr. Lindsay as Headmaster, things changed a lot. He was a forward-thinking Head.

For many of the boys, the hairdresser is somebody to talk to. You have to listen and share their family problems and their homesickness. We also visit some Nursing Homes and the housebound. We are their contact with the outside world— often the only person they've seen all week. It's very rewarding.

Hair styles have become much more casual and natural. In the mid '60's it was the beehive style for ladies. For men, the Beatles brought in longer hair. There have been great advances in colouring. We match the colour with the eyebrows."

POSTMAN

Malvern postmen are to my mind a special breed. They carry heavy packs up and down steep hills and long drives. But nowadays, on hot summer days they are permitted to wear navy blue shorts. This would have amazed and shocked their Victorian counterparts!

Alan Tyler was postman in West Malvern for nine years. He now walks three miles a day—to keep fit! "When you've walked 12 miles a day for your work, it's no good putting your feet up!" he said.

"I remember some bad winters," he added. "1947, 1963 (the worst) and 1981-82. In 1981, I slipped on ice with my load of 35 pounds' weight. The letters scattered. I picked them up not noticing that I had gashed my arm and blood had dripped over the letters. I wiped them and apologised to the recipients. 'We don't mind that', they replied, 'but how's your arm?' A kind lady put some plaster on my arm.

Once, coming down a steep snowy slope in a West Malvern garden, I slipped and clung to a fence—which gave way! I picked myself up, **and** the fence, and I repositioned it.

People used to say, 'Why don't you wear mitts?' But I would always reply, 'If I did that, and pushed open a wet gate, I'd get the **addresses** wet and unreadable.' It was hard enough to read them on dark mornings, even **with** a torch."

POST OFFICE CLERK

Ivy Pitt told me: "I worked at the Post Office in Great Malvern. To save time, I used to walk over the hills from West Malvern to my work in Great Malvern. I went up by the Dingle. It only took me about a quarter of an hour.

In summer I would set off at 3 a.m. and be at work at half-past three. I used to hear a little bird 'peeping', and another one and another one. When I got down to St. Ann's Delight, by the little zig-zag path, the whole dawn chorus was singing then. It was lovely!

I remember seeing a man asleep on the hills. I was frightened, but I did manage to go past him without waking him up. But going down the 99 steps, I felt I had no bones in my legs.

The Postmaster called me in and said, 'Ivy, I didn't realise I had a lady walking over the hill. I can't let you walk again.' So, a person was detailed to pick me up in a van and take me down to work early in the morning.

I worked there for 4 years in the Second World War. I used to take telegrams and registered parcels. We had telegrams in code from TRE, the radar establishment. And lots of telegrams of bereavement. Then the men came back from the war and took over their old jobs again.

It was wonderful working in the Post Office at Christmas, 'cos everyone was so friendly."

MILKMAN

Reg Green related: "In the 1920's, I heard that Mr. Medcalf, a Guarlford farmer, required a milkman to deliver milk in Malvern. I did this job for 21 years. At the time, I thought it great fun to work on a farm. I was very fond of horses and thought it great to be driving a fast pony.

My job as a milkman was a seven-days-a-week job. I had to start work at 6 o'clock in the morning. My first duty was to milk four or five cows. No milking machines in those days!

I well remember my first attempt at milking a cow. A large shorthorn named Daisy, always took a dislike to strangers. A well-placed kick knocked me backwards, with the bucket and stool on top of me!

The milk was put through a cotton-wool strainer, then straight into the churns. It was then ready for the customer. Housewives often refused to have the milk unless it was still warm from the cow. That's how they knew it really was fresh milk.

After a quick breakfast in the farmhouse kitchen, I had to be out on the road by 7.30 a.m. I had to ladle the milk out of churns into the housewives' jugs or basins, in half-pints, pints or quarts. The price was about 3 pence per pint.

Having delivered in the Barnards Green and Poolbrook area, I returned to the farm to wash the churns and cans. After the mid-day break, I set off again for the afternoon delivery of milk. I finished work at 5.30 p.m."

PHYSIOTHERAPIST

"During Malvern Festivals in the 1930's, several of the actors were patients of mine," said Gwen Forster. "The husband of Dame Laura Knight, the artist, was one. Another of them was Helena Pickard, the actress wife of Sir Cedric Hardwicke. I recall their little son, Edward, sitting at the foot of the bed, while I was giving massage to his mother. He was chatting away to me. Now I see Edward Hardwicke on television, quite a lot."

GAMEKEEPER

Rose Nash told me: "Mr. Green organised the shoots on Madresfield estate. My husband, Harold, helped Mr. Green in the woods, rearing pheasants. Harold was given a few pheasants' eggs, one day. He put them under a hen, and we reared quite a few pheasants.

I had to help him de-beak them. You had a little round battery thing. When it got hot, you blunted the tips of their beaks, so that they didn't peck one another. They are cannibals once they start."

PLUCKING POULTRY

Reg Green recalled: "My grandparents lived at Guarlford, in a small cottage on the Clevelode Road. A regular occupation for my grandmother at Michaelmas and Christmas was plucking poultry for the local farmers. This went on for two or three days at a time.

It meant that there was always a good supply of goose-down for the making of feather beds, which were popular in those days. As a boy, I found it rather wonderful to snuggle into a featherbed made of goose-down. Not very healthy perhaps, but always snug and warm!"

IN SERVICE

Ellen Hymas related: "My mother, at the age of 13, went in

service to a Guest House in Westgate Street, Hereford. She had to get up at 6 a.m., blacklead the grate, scrub the outside step and polish the brass plate on the door. Then she had to make a cup of tea for her Mistress and take it up to her. The Mistress would then get up and make breakfast for the guests."

Win Foster said: "I went to work for Mrs. Courtney Lord. She lived in Farley Road, Malvern Link. They bought me an alarm clock to help me get up in the mornings. I had to wear a uniform and answer the door.

Mrs. Courtney Lord was a real lady. I had to help her dress. For dinner, she always had a finger bowl, to dip her fingers in and wipe them on her serviette. She had a lot of silver and nice china."

Kath Hill recalled: "As Tweenie (between maid) I had to wash and iron the underwear and white silk tennis dresses of my Mistress. She played a lot of tennis. There were lots of tennis parties at the house.

One day, when I was 15, using a flat iron (no electric irons then) I scorched a silk petticoat on the front. I confessed to my Mistress, feeling *very* sorry. She replied, 'Well, it's done now. You've learnt your lesson. I'm going to give you a new lace top to sew on after you've cut out the burned piece.'

Next, I went to work for two ladies in Graham Road. But I had to carry the coal and wood for fires in both lounges up from the cellar. I was not strong enough for this, and I pointed this out to them.

'We'll get someone to help you', they replied. They got the gardener from next door—Reg, my future husband! I saved up five shillings per week for 6 years for my wedding dress, my mother's dress, and the reception."

TELEPRINTER

Frances Milsom told me: "In the 1930's I worked for Babcock and Wilcock in the Black Country. I became Head of the Typing Pool, with ten girls under me. I was the first in that district to learn the teleprinter.

Everyone used to come to see my typing on the teleprinter. You could just touch a button and you were through to America. Then came the Second World War and it all had to be very secret."

TELEGRAPHIST

Helen Mooney recalled: "My father worked at the Post Office, with the most irregular hours. He was an expert telegraphist. He worked on the old-fashioned keyboard. This was the 'Dot and Dash' Morse code for sending telegraphs and receiving them.

In the First World War, my father was in the Royal Engineers as telegraphist. We scarcely saw him for four years because he was in France."

MONUMENTAL SCULPTURE

"I went to work with my father," said Eric Jones. "I've worked on Malvern Priory, and churches at Mathon, Welland and Longdon, doing repairs. We made gravestones and did the lettering as well.

We took the top off Longdon Church. We had to have the weather cock gilded. They got a little girl to go up there afterwards and fix the weather cock. She was about 13—from the local school, and she didn't seem a bit afraid. I went up behind her right to the top of the spire.

We experience the swaying of a church tower when they ring the bells. I never did like that! But if it didn't make that movement, the tower would collapse."

DRESSMAKER

Austin Hartwright's mother was a dressmaker. During the First World War, Austin would be sent, as a schoolboy, to a house in Avenue Road, Malvern, with a large box of finished dressmaking. His mother would say to him, 'Wait for the box!' (meaning the payment too.)

But Austin would often have to return **without** the payment on which his mother relied so much to feed her 8 children. On his return, he would see his mother's face saddened.

Bridget Fish told me: "My husband's mother was Frances Fish ('Franny'). She was an excellent dressmaker. From an early age, she was a seamstress at Warwick House, Malvern. She had to pay for her 5 years of apprenticeship. She worked at Warwick House for 15 years.

She regularly made bride's dresses and dresses for two bridesmaids within seven days. She would sew all through the night to get them finished. In the war years, some bridal dresses were made out of parachute silk. In wartime, with clothes rationing, you were glad to have old clothes altered to fit, or re-styled, and Frances was very good at alterations."

LEATHER WORKER

Hilda Beale told me: "I worked in Blackfriars, Worcester, for

Luxton Gloves. During the war we made gloves for Marks and Spencers—beautiful gloves, fur backed. There were a lot of outside glove makers around Worcester. It had been a home industry in villages around Worcester for two centuries.

Then I came to Malvern to work for Leathercraft. We made army jerkins for soldiers and flying suits for the Royal Air Force during the war. They were very strong and well-lined.

Leathercraft was at Link Top in the old police station. There were old police cells there and a lot of rats. Mr. and Mrs. Stevens used to keep Leathercraft. Mrs. Stevens bred rabbits. She used the rabbit skins for lining the gloves."

CUSTOS AT MALVERN PRIORY

Charles Smith recollected: "In the 1920's, Sundays were very quiet. No shops were open. Sunday was respected. As a boy, I was in the choir at St. Andrew's church, Poolbrook.

One day, the verger there, said to me, 'How would you like to blow the organ (it was the old pump action then) and ring the bell?' I thought that would be glorious. I was only a lad. It sowed the seeds for my future job! I went to church. Then I rebelled. But I came back.

Years later, in 1964, I started work in Malvern Priory. I became Custos and spent 15 very happy years there. I enjoyed meeting people. It was a lovely peaceful place to work in—in solitude. And we had a lot of visitors from abroad. I've been up the tower many times. My legs ache! I used to wind the clock every Thursday morning, and you had to go up there to do that. But you get used to it."

ERRAND BOY

In the 1920's and '30's, schoolboys aged 10 and upwards, earned pocket money as errand boys for local shopkeepers. Either they were lent bikes for this purpose, or they walked. Housewives made sure that errand boys did not starve!

Francis Bird told me: "I did the newspaper round for Granny Andrews in Poolbrook. I fetched the papers from the railway station. My first call was Mrs. Cotterell. She was a laundress. Always ironing, she was. She would give me a cup of soup if it was cold weather. Her house was beautifully warm."

Disney Reynolds said: "I used to take round parcels for a lady dressmaker in Newtown Road. I had to take a parcel to a Miss Houghton. She had as her companion one of the Sisters from the Convent. In church, those Sisters used to keep an eye on us boys.

Anyway, I took this parcel. The cook there knew me. She said, 'Step inside!' But Miss Houghton came in and exclaimed, 'What are you doing in my house? You're a tradesman. You get outside!' I would be about ten then.

Another place I went was in Como Road, for Mrs. Brewer, the dressmaker, who had a nice apartment there. I used to go to the front door. *She* was kind. She always said, 'Would you like to go round to the back door where there will be a supper for you?"

Arthur Russell told me: "My first job was at Lygon Pharmacy at Link Top as general errand boy. My mother always gave me a good breakfast—bacon, egg, and fried bread. She said, 'Always have a good breakfast, son—in case you don't get anything else to eat all day.'

And there was Mrs. Sillman. She was the housekeeper to

Mr. John Need, the chemist, my employer. She looked after me very well. At 10 o'clock I had to cook breakfast for her and Mr. Need—and have one myself! so I had two breakfasts!

Then I would go out with my satchel delivering medicines up Hornyold Road and Blackmore Road. I went home to dinner. At 4 o'clock I had to get tea for Mr. Need. Mrs. Sillman said, 'You're a growing lad. You want feeding'. So, I had tea there too!"

11 ~ We Went Shopping

· ·

In company with many other spa towns, Great Malvern cherished its old established shops.

STATELY SHOPS OF MALVERN

Warwick House

This venerable shop had a long and noble pedigree. Warwick House began in 1833 and reigned as a much-esteemed department store until 1992.

"I always bought my hats at Warwick House," said Elizabeth Guise Berrow. "I knew Gertrude Mitchell, the owner, when she had a shop in Worcester. She always stocked nice quality things."

Lilian Drinkwater told me: "Warwick House was known as Cox and Painter's in my day. We just looked in the windows and that's all! Their clothes were not the kind of thing you would wear every day." Dorothy Jones went even further. "We said they were for 'frumpy' people! There were big hats with feathers in their windows."

Joan Green, however, related to me the inside story of this famous shop. Her memories were vivid, as she worked there for 33 years. "I began at Warwick House in November 1949, and I was always happy there until I left in 1982.

It was extremely prosperous in 1949. Our customers came

mostly from the Hereford area—county people. Farmers' wives from Herefordshire would come in for their winter clothes, particularly after hop picking was finished. Some customers came down regularly from Birmingham and from the Cotswolds. One Cotswolds lady would buy five expensive hats at a time.

Weekends were very very busy in term time. In those days, pupils at the College didn't go home as often as now. So, their parents came down to see them and shopped at Warwick House.

Some customers would only request a certain assistant to serve them. They would make appointments for this. For instance, Dame Laura Knight, the artist, would only have Mrs. Gertrude Mitchell herself to serve her when choosing a hat.

People would shop for clothes for special occasions, like the Cheltenham Gold Cup, Ascot, Wimbledon, and Royal visits.

I started in Millinery. After a while I became buyer in Accessories Departments—handbags, gloves, scarves. Later, I was buyer for Millinery and then for Lingerie. We were called upon to go to the Fashion Depts. bringing the accessories for customers to choose and match up.

Handbags were framed at one time with handles. Then they became shoulder bags. In my day lizard and crocodile were used. It would be frowned upon now, wouldn't it! We were thrilled when we saw the crocodile bag, because, of course, the price would be good!

For hats, we had our own milliner, Miss Darling. Everyone knew Miss Darling. She would make hats for weddings and do bridal headdresses. And we bought London hats. Over the years, hats have changed. Softer materials came in—velvet, and crinoline straws in the summer.

I lived in over the shop. A dozen or more staff lived in then. This went on till 1951. There was a Housekeeper—a Mrs. Racetti. She was an Austrian refugee. And her husband and mother lived there too. We had a morning cook to cook us breakfast and another cook to cook us supper for about 6.30 p.m.

I came from Ombersley. Another girl came from Bridgenorth. Several came from Ledbury or Castlemorton way. Some girls had always lived in. They were much older than me and had obviously been in business all their lives.

The food was very good. I had my own bedroom. The bedrooms became showrooms eventually. If you were out late, you had to ring a bell. But I wasn't one who went to the dances at the Winter Gardens.

On winter evenings, we would talk, listen to the radio (no T.V. then) or go to the pictures. After supper, in the summer, one girl and I would walk all over Malvern. We would go on the hills.

We closed on a Thursday afternoon. Then it changed to Wednesdays. Every 6 weeks you got a Saturday and a Monday. We worked till 5.30 p.m. on Saturdays."

In the early 1960's, when Warwick House was at its zenith, the shop employed an impressively large number of staff. The office alone employed 13 people. There were 6 porters. There was a large furs department. 8 fitters worked there to adjust clothes for customers, ready for the 14 dressmakers to sew, or the 12 people in the Tailoring Dept. to work on. The School Uniform Dept. employed 4 assistants. There was also a Hairdressing Salon—Victor Coiffures.

Joan Green continues her intriguing memories: "Rosie Beames was our wonderful dressmaker who made wonderful wedding dresses. She was always a little bit superstitious. She would never finish off the wedding dress till after the last bridal fitting. There would be one little button to sew on or a little loop to put on the train. That was a whole day's visit for the bride, her mother, and the bridesmaids, in the fitting room.

There were 4 or 5 workrooms with people altering school uniforms. Before the First World War there were great numbers of girls in workrooms on long tables using big flat irons and treadle sewing machines.

We supplied school uniforms for Malvern Girls' College, Ellerslie, Lawnside and Douglas House, but never for Malvern College. In September, at the start of the new school year, it was bedlam for a few days in the shop with parents and new pupils. And there were many girls from abroad. The present girls don't look so smart!

Gertrude Mitchell was an excellent businesswoman. She had brought all her Worcester shop staff over to Warwick House. And she started the man's shop on Bellevue Terrace. She owned Mount Pleasant hotel too.

"Malvern is run by women" proclaimed the national press in the 1950's. There was Miss Newth with her bookshop, Miss King, Editor of the Malvern Gazette, and Mrs. Mitchell at Warwick House. She employed some excellent window dressers—and she lived to be 100.

I enjoyed the changeover to Gieves and Hawkes in 1978. We had to send everything to their headquarters in Portsmouth to get orders passed. But our shop was too feminine for them because they are famous mainly for being military tailors. But we heard some nice tales about what they did in Savile Row keeping the uniforms for officers.

Warwick House finished because of the change in fashion

and the attitude of customers. The fashions in children's clothes changed to washable dungarees, jeans, and T-shirts.

But I shall always remember the 150th Anniversary of Warwick House in 1983, when Princess Anne attended our grand Fashion Show."

May Sadler worked in Warwick House as seamstress for a total of 32 years. But she did not live *in*. May did alterations to school uniforms. When Gieves and Hawkes took over, she made cloaks for naval officers' wives for Naval balls. "They were navy blue with red satin linings," she recalled. "Gieves and Hawkes were tailors to Admiral Nelson and have always been associated with the Royal Navy."

Let May Sadler pronounce the epitaph for the flagship, Warwick House: "When the receivers came, in 1992, the end was sad. With all my friends gone, I was left alone in an eerie, empty shop. I had to complete the wedding dresses which were still in the cupboards. I had always felt happy there. It took me a long time to get over the closure of Warwick House."

Brays of Malvern

This respected and highly valued shop celebrated its centenary in 1995 and is still going strong. H. Bray & Co. opened in 1895 on the present premises at No. 1 The Promenade. In 1903, the shop was styled 'Tailors, Clothiers, Juvenile Outfitters', and the window surrounds were in polished mahogany. The clothing on sale was for men and boys only in those days.

Tailoring staff were probably employed on the premises almost from the start, and this continued right until the 1960's. The workroom finally closed in January 1967. For a few years a small number of staff 'lived in' on the premises, sleeping on the top floor and taking their meals in the end room of the basement.

In 1931, No. 4 The Promenade opened as a Ladies' Department. From early days, Brays offered deliveries of customers' purchases, the earliest form of transport being by carrier's bicycle.

School outfitting played a significant part in the firm's business from the earliest days. Over the years, they supplied boys' preparatory schools like The Wells House, Hillstone School, The Downs School, The Elms School, Croftdown and Hillside Schools, and many other schools much further afield. The sale of luggage and leather goods has continued steadily over the years.

Loyal staff at Brays have given decades of long and devoted service. They have received many deserving tributes from satisfied customers.

Mr. C.R. Davis, who was Managing Director of the firm from 1936 to 1981, recollected some fascinating memories of Brays, his father's shop, as it was in 1914: "When I began my apprenticeship under my father in 1914, we opened the shop each day at 8 o'clock. We closed at 7.30 p.m. on Monday, Tuesday, and Wednesday. Thursday was the half-day. But on Friday we did not close until 8 p.m. On Saturday we were open until 10 p.m.

Our dress then—black jackets, dark trousers, black ties, white stiff collars, and tailcoats for the senior salesmen. We sold corduroy trousers for the working man. Prices 15 shillings and sixpence, best quality 18 shillings and sixpence. Stiff white collars and cuffs were on sale then, and also nightshirts for men.

Window dressing in my early days was a major operation. It would often take two to three days to dress one window.

The idea was to pack as much stock into the window as was physically possible—otherwise customers would think you did not stock the very items they wanted to buy!

My father would dress the window. It was my job to wait upon him. The window had to be cleaned and the gas lamps attended to. Numerous brass rods had to be dusted and placed on brackets reaching from floor to ceiling. On these the goods were hung. Each garment had a large price ticket and a descriptive ticket— 'Style and Quality', 'Just Received', or 'As Now Worn'.

The customer of those days was bowed in and bowed out, always addressed as 'Sir' or 'Madam', and always offered a chair—high bentwood type with cane seat. Certain customers would not be served by any but the proprietor.

Hosiery and underwear was kept in parcels, not openly displayed. So, after a long session with a fussy customer, there were numerous packets to be tied up again in only one way as laid down. Clothing was not hung on rails as it is nowadays. Everything had to be folded and packed away according to regulations.

Apprenticeship was usually for three years and was very hard, but very thorough. But during that time, all the apprentice received was two or three shillings a week pocket money."

John Stainer, who gave 44 years' service to Brays used to tell this story of a lady and her small son. She came into the shop, complaining indignantly about a school sweater she had purchased not long previously. It had pulled apart at the seams. Stainer took one look at the sweater and rounded on the boy. "You had a fight, didn't you?" "Yes," came the meek reply. ***You never told me that!*** exclaimed his mother. End of complaint.

Over the past century, Brays have received numerous letters of appreciation from their grateful customers:

"May I say again how much I appreciate the excellent service Brays give us: it is always a delight to arrive at such an oasis of calm, and your stocks seem inexhaustible!"

"I have much pleasure in writing this letter of thanks for the suede jacket which arrived in Gillingham on Friday, the day prior to my return to France. It is unusual, in these days of indolence, to find people with initiative and drive who actually seek to please and sell."

"I am most impressed by your kindness and efficiency, in buying and having delivered to the school for me, a sledge for our small boy. In fact, you quite astonished me. Brays has always been famous in my family for service—now it is even more so."

"Well done. Thank heavens there is still private enterprise, complete with kindness and sincerity."

Brays can feel justly proud of such testimonies.

Cridlan and Walker

This is Great Malvern's oldest shop. It was established in 1830, close to the Abbey Gateway, and is still thriving. The original owners, J&B Walker, were specialists in Welsh Mutton, which was much served by Dr. Wilson to his patients at nearby Graefenberg House, his Water Cure establishment, in the 1840's.

J&B Walker also sold Poultry, Cream Cheese, and Fresh Butter. For many years, the butchers in this shop hung their meat outside, on hooks on the Abbey Gateway adjoining.

Were the original Victorian owner to return, he would be astonished to see on sale today Lamb stuffed with Cranberry and Orange, Pork stuffed with Plum and Ginger, Pork sausages flavoured with Apple and Cider, and Beef sausages flavoured with Guinness or Worcester sauce.

Tipping and Morris

This high-quality grocer's began as an Italian Warehouse in the 1850's, at Mount Pleasant Place, near to the Belle Vue Hotel. They specialised in teas, coffees, cocoas, and wines.

"In the 1930's and 1940's it was like Jacksons of Piccadilly," said Louise Lenton. "Mr. Lloyd Morris, the proprietor, always wore a lounge suit and always greeted his customers. He was a smart, military sort of man."

Disney Reynolds told me: "I went into the grocery trade at Tipping and Morris. I had to work hard, mind you. I had a very good job there for nearly 30 years. I knew the senior man. He was a Trinity Church sidesman. I think it was the fact that he knew me that I got the job. I was buying bacon. The bacon firms came to me in the shop, and the cheese merchants.

When Malvern Girls' College opened the Domestic Science blocks at Parkfield, of course, it was the cat's whiskers for our shop. Because they bought the best of everything. The girls had to make different things in Cookery. Every term, we showed the girls round the shop, so that they knew what we sold. Of course, all the Malvern tradesmen have done well out of the boarding schools.

We supplied all the hotels. The Abbey Hotel was the cat's whiskers. They had page boys there then. The Foley Arms bought a lot of fresh ground coffee every week from us.

During the Second World War, I was helping in the Tipping and Morris shop. It was one Friday afternoon, when a great big, tall fellow came in. He was a naval officer. He had three girls from the Girls' College with him, and his wife.

155

He was looking at me intently. 'Oh,' he said, 'You're still here? Remember me? I'm Todd, House number 7. I was educated at Malvern College. Here are my three daughters.' So, you had quite a few people who remembered us. It was 'Yes, Madam', and 'No Sir', in the old days."

Kendalls

In 1852, David Kendall had started his shop, in the blossoming spa of Malvern, on the corner of Church Street and Graham Road. A large notice in the shop's window had stated, 'We sell mantles and hats, blankets and sheets, and every article for the hydropathic treatment, including unshrinkable undergarments.'

"It was a wonderful shop!" enthused Ornella Benson. "When Kendalls went, Malvern began to die. Kendalls catered for the middle market. They stocked everything—shoes, underwear, linen, haberdashery, fashions, and materials for sewing and knitting. And your payment was sent spinning in boxes on wires, above the counters. Being situated at the bottom of the hill, in Church Street, Kendalls was a very accessible shop." For their annual Blanket Sale in September, bales of blankets would arrive from the Witney Blanket Company.

Burley's Hairdressing Salon

Burley's were tobacconists as well as hairdressers in the early days. Harry Burley's accounts book, dated February 1920, shows takings for one day as:

Ladies Salon: 2 shillings and 6 pence

Gents Salon: 17 shillings and $5^1/_2$ pence

Repair of Umbrellas (by Sidney Hood in cellar):
12 shillings and 6 pence

Harry and his son, Dennis Burley, made up their own preparations for hair. They always had a lot of customers in September, at the time of the Worcester Three Choirs' Festival.

The Hairdresser's BIBLE was a thick tome: The Art and Craft of Hairdressers by Gilbert Foan, 1930. It shows numerous photos of current hair styles for ladies entitled: The Eton Crop; The Bachelor Girl; The Chic; The Lily.

In the 1930's it was fashionable for women to have A Water Wave, A Marcel Wave, or a Shingle with Rolled Curls. The Burleys have been customers of one firm, named CRISCUOLO, ever since 1921. This firm supplies side combs and are under Appointment to Her Majesty the Queen Mother, to this day.

The Bluebird Tea Rooms

The Indian and China teas shop was where the Bluebird Tea Rooms is now. The Bluebird Tea Rooms was established in 1913. They specialised in tea. Troyte Griffith, the Malvern architect, could often be seen in these tea rooms with Sir Edward Elgar, his friend.

The Dorothy Café

Louise Lenton told me: "That café was run by a Swiss lady, Anna Schneider, whose brother owned a café in Cheltenham. The Swiss cakes in Dorothy's came from Cheltenham. Next door, was a very long and narrow little pub called The Fermor."

Dorothy Jones has nostalgic memories about the Dorothy Café. "After going to the cinema in Malvern, we'd have tea at the Dorothy. They had beautiful chocolate cakes; Swiss made. Sometimes, even now, I dream I'm in that cafe with Mum."

F.L. Cox & Son

This is another old family firm which is still thriving. It was established on its present site in Newtown Road in 1883, by Florence Louise Burston, the great grandmother of the present owner, David Cox. It was opened as a general store, selling clothing, china, bedding, flooring, footwear, and haberdashery. At around the turn of the century, the focus changed to clothing.

David Cox's daughter explains their continuing success: "We always pride ourselves on personal service and attention to detail. These are essentials of successful retailing."

Margaret Hands told me: "My grandmother went to Cox's to shop. She paid into a club there and had the money out every Christmas, towards clothes, shoes, and towels. My mother was in it too. Now *I'm* in the Club. It is still run by the sons and grandsons." (This was told me in 1997). Cox's have always kept a good relationship with their customers.

Arthur Russell had praise too for this very old shop. "We used to get all our clothing for the family there. They measured us for our suits in those days. The old shop sign, 'BESPOKE TAILOR', is still up there, I think, on the wall of the shop. I always like to deal with local firms, because you haven't far to go to put things right."

SMALLER SHOPS IN GREAT MALVERN

Violets

It was a sweet shop on Bellevue Terrace. Louise Lenton told me: "'Violets' was run by a Mrs. Porter. Then Eileen Morgan took it over in about 1939. It was a pretty little shop, with posies of violets. What you bought was wrapped in a special way. The Mount Pleasant annexed this shop when it closed."

Yvonne Hodges added: "The fretwork 'fringe' or frill of latticework which bordered the shelves in this shop was very distinctive."

Morleys

"It was owned by Mr. Morley who was lost in the Titanic disaster," said Louise Lenton. "There were mirrors all round the walls. They sold specialised chocolates, loose, on trays. You chose one of this and two of those—chocolates decorated with little violets and roses."

Winifred's

Margaret Davis recalled: "It was near Kendall's. I worked in Winifred's for 28 years. A lot of people remember me. I had to go in the Land Army during the war. But I went back in the shop afterwards. We sold wools, embroidery things, underwear, and dresses. It was a very good little business."

Davis Fish and Game

"Fishy" Davis was a shopkeeper of importance in the town. He sold fish and game on the corner of Church Street with Graham Road in the Exchange buildings. The Telephone Exchange was above.

Disney Reynolds recollected: "'Fishy' Davis had a very good voice. He sang in the Madresfield Choral Society, along with singers from very distinguished Malvern families. It was unheard of in those days of the 1930's, for a tradesman to sing in such an elite choir. But *he* was in it!"

The Maypole

Ellen Hymas recalled: "We used to get our lovely butter from there, and marmalade. They would slice the butter and pat it up with wooden butter pats."

Piper's Penny Bazaar

"That Penny Bazaar enthralled me as a child," said Mary Wells. "A penny went quite a long way then. It was opposite the Foley Arms Hotel up some black and white steps. They sold all kinds of things—candles, potholders of padded cloth to lift the kettle from the open fire, handkerchiefs, shoelaces, pencils, crayons, and little dolls."

"I liked to spend my penny there," added Ellen Hymas. "Once I bought two little celluloid dolls to fit in a matchbox—a black doll and a white doll. I took them home to show my mother. But my brother said, 'I'll show you a trick'. He put them through the mangle, and they came out flat! He was a torment! But he gave me a penny to get another box of dolls."

MALVERN LINK

In the 1920's, Malvern Link was a village and very very pretty," said Helen Cutler. "We lived at the Dairy there. Two walnut trees lined the road near where the Co-op supermarket now is. An open stream ran where their wall is, then it went underground. All along Richmond Road were flowering almond trees. Lime trees lined the road leading to Great Malvern."

Pembridge, Hatter and Hosier

Mr. Pembridge sold men's hats. His shop was where Barclay's

Bank is now. He was the Secretary of the Madresfield Show for many years. His wife was Nurse to the Lygon children of Madresfield Court.

Fillmore's

"It was a charming old shop", Frank Bowers remembered. "It was a sweet shop and tobacconist's with a huge chestnut tree outside. And they sold snuff from barrels as well as in tins."

Mary Wells added: "You could purchase your maggots and fishing bait there, as well as fishing licences for the Severn and Teme."

Joan Smith remembered two other shops in Malvern Link. "Miss Dutson had a sweet shop, where Celia Bishop's is now. Miss Dutson's trade was so marvellous that she bought the house next door, now the Flower shop, to set up her second sweet shop. Fancy sweet shops being so busy then!"

Mr. and Mrs. Hunter had a clothes shop. As a child, I had a coat made there. I remember it was green tweed with a black velvet collar. I've always been fond of green. They made to measure in those days. People all shopped locally then."

Price's

"You could buy anything in the clothes line there," recalled Margaret Hands. "The windows were stacked with stuff. The prices were in three farthings—one and eleven pence three farthings. But instead of giving you one farthing change, they gave you a packet of pins. It kept the Sheffield steel industry going! I bought all my babies' smocks and dresses there, little socks, and shoes. It was a very useful shop."

Francis of Malvern

This furniture firm was founded in 1933, when William Guy Francis battled through hard times to create today's extensive business. His son, Derek Francis, the present owner, was born and bred in Malvern. His proud boast is that, "We have supplied furniture to almost every town in England and Wales, and we are now the largest retailer in Malvern."

"There are two things I always say you should spend a lot of money on. One is your bed, and the other is your shoes. Because if you are not in one, you're in the other."

This is the wise saying of Bryan Savage, Director, and Manager of the Bedding department. He has worked for Francis for 30 years. "Francis now sells more single beds than any other furniture. Mattresses are now in lighter colours—cream and beige.

Teak is still popular for tables and chairs, with heat resistant surfaces instead of Formica. Customers prefer local scenes, for pictures. For carpets, plain colours are now preferred—greens, fawns, pinks.

Deliveries of furniture can be tricky—or hilarious! Three wardrobes once slid down a hill at Colwall. One day, in a gale, a wardrobe was blown off the van and careered down the street, flapping its doors, like wings!"

Derek Francis told me: "Three generations of Francis have been upholsterers. My grandfather came from Derbyshire, to be upholsterer at Powick Asylum. My father, living in Powick village, saw the first motor car to travel from Worcester to Malvern."

NEWTOWN ROAD

Eileen Hymas remembered some shops in Newtown Road. "Turner's, the newspaper shop sold briar pipes and little white clay pipes. Mr. Burston sold shoes. Mr. Cullen mended shoes. In Miss Lea's sweet shop, we used to get little V-shaped bags of mixed sweets for one halfpenny. All the odd sweets left over. I remember Humbugs, Liquorice Allsorts, Jelly Babies and Raspberry Drops."

BARNARDS GREEN

Joan Preece told me: "I remember the old-fashioned draper's, owned by Mrs. Johnson. She would stand just inside her shop, until she was in her 90's. The shop had long counters and tall chairs for customers. She stocked 'combs' (combinations) and old-fashioned corsets. It was quite a thriving little business until it ceased in the early 1980's.

Hunts' ~ Fruits, Flowers, Vegetables and Game

John Hunt has never retired. He was plucking Mallard (wild duck) when I met him in the shop. "It all began in 1907", he said. "My father started the business in Court Road, which is now Hunts' Flower Shop.

Our shop was originally a dairy. My father had a very big milk round. We still supply all the hotels with our produce. They are a flourishing and regular trade.

Supplying game began in 1948. It used to come from London then. Now it's all local. Lord Hambro at Dumbleton has a very big estate. We have all our pheasants from him. Our pheasants are going to Monmouth today, to a delicatessen.

Other game we supply? Partridges, pigeons, venison, geese, quails and quail eggs and Christmas turkeys."

LITTLE SHOPS FLOURISHED IN THE OLD DAYS

"Great Malvern was like a foreign country to us, when we lived in Quest Hills Road, Malvern Link," said Win Foster. "Because Quest Hills Road was self-contained. There was a wet fish shop and a fried fish shop, a Post Office and shop, a grocer, a shoe repairer, a hairdresser and two pubs. We had no reason to go to Great Malvern—except for going to the pictures (cinema)."

"The village shop?" said Meriel Hodgetts in Upper Welland. "To people like me who have no car, the village shop is still the biggest lifeline there is. We still have a Post Office (in 1998). It's a wonderful shop, with a delicatessen counter. I get all I want there. We rely on it for everything."

Margaret Davis recalled: "We used to have in Upper Welland a little shop that sold corn and feed stuff for pigs and poultry—and paraffin. There were several little shops here. And Malvern Wells had everything—a doctor, a chemist, two grocers, a butcher, a hairdresser, draper, ironmonger, and so on. We were better supplied *then* than now."

Elsie Godsell recollected a similar wide variety of little shops in Colwall—and two banks. "It is sad to see shops closing. But we are very grateful for the shops we still have," she added.

"Armstrongs was a very nice draper's shop and ironmonger's in Colwall. It was run by three sisters—Miss Gertie, Miss Ethel, and Miss Gladys. The shop and house had been built by their father when they moved here in the early 1900's. After Ethel died, Gladys still carried on till she was 90."

And the little shops obligingly kept open till late at night, as Arthur Russell recalled: "One Saturday, I worked on till nine o'clock at night. They paid me and I went up to Mrs. Hart at the little comer shop on the Quest Hills Road. She always kept open till 10 p.m.

I went up to get a tin of beef for dinner. And she had a chicken, costing £2. I said, 'I'll toss a coin with you. If I win, you can sell it to me for £1.' It was a bit of fun really. It was 'Tails' and I *did* win. So, it was a bargain. And I went home with the chicken, like a dog with six tails wagging!"

12 ~ We Went to Church

• •

Malvern has always had a broad spectrum and diversity of churches. Nowadays, its churches are more open for secular activities and more ready to co-operate with each other.

SCALING NEW HEIGHTS

A young lady who sang in the choir,
Had a voice that rose higher and higher.
Till one terrible night,
It rose out of sight,
Then came down to rest on the spire.

(From a Malvern Women's Institute
Limerick Competition)

"I sang in the choir at St. Matthias church", said Reginald Hall-Robinson. "I was **made** to go to church **and** Sunday School. Our mothers were in the Mothers' Union. We didn't say Grace at meals, but my mother was a pretty religious sort. As soon as I hadn't got to go—I didn't go!"

Madge Howard Davies told me: "At St. Matthias, we had over 20 boys in the choir in the '60's and '70's. Now there are none. The boys all go to sport on Sunday mornings. So, our choir is largely adults."

Peter Treherne recollected: "As children, we had to go to

Sunday School every Sunday afternoon while my parents had a rest. In fact, we went to church three times every Sunday."

Disney Reynolds had happier memories of Sunday School. "Trinity Church Parish Hall was full, every Sunday at 10 o'clock. The Senior children went up top and the Juniors at the bottom. Our teachers were the Miss Fittons from Fairlea—the friends of Sir Edward Elgar.

We boys were in Miss Claire Fitton's Bible class for years. We had to learn the Collect every Sunday. You had to recite it out loud. Then you went into church and came out before the Sermon.

Holy Trinity church had a big choir—about 30 to 40 men and boys. I got in the choir as a very young boy and eventually became Head Choirboy."

Freda Morris recalled: "When I was 19 years old, I was a Sunday School teacher. We went down to the Convent of the Holy Name once a week to get our lessons. We used to creep into church after the sermon. I had 14 children in my class and there were 3 classes. Sisters from the Convent came up to help. We had Sunday School parties in the field by the Convent."

Dorothy Jones remembered: "We had a big Sunday School at Somers Park Methodist Church. For Whitsuntide, we wore our white dresses and black patent shoes. We sang excerpts from The Messiah on the stage in church.

For our Christmas party, our teachers, the Miss Thomases, always made boiled sweets and wrapped them in bags. The sweets and oranges were put in a big clothes basket. We sang 'A Hunting we will go' … When you were caught, you were given your bag of sweets and your orange."

Dorothy recalled Sunday School outings to Evesham, Bishops Cleeve, and by train to Barry Island.

SOME MEMORABLE PRIESTS

The Reverend David Scotcher

At St. Matthias he was well known for his forthright sermons, and woe betide if you didn't pay attention.

Freda Morris remembered: "Father Scotcher used to say, 'A good 'Damn' is better than 'Tut Tut' any day!' And do you know that has always stayed in my mind, the way he shouted it out. He would thump the pulpit when he was preaching. As little girls, we were terrified of him."

Minna Bowers told me: "Father Scotcher liked to play a prank on Nurse Edwards. She was the District Nurse and a maternity nurse. She was a great church person and rode a bike. If ever Father Scotcher saw her bike outside somebody's house, he would move it to two or three roads away. The Nurse would find it eventually."

The Reverend Maynard Smith

"He was our Vicar at Holy Trinity church", said Disney Reynolds. "He and his brother were really High Church. We had the Litany every other Sunday, as regular as clockwork. You had to fast in Lent.

The Vicar had three maids, a cook, and a gardener. They used to have a ton of coal every week, at the Vicarage, from Cannock Chase. There would be great big fires in their studies in the Vicarage.

We went to the Vicarage for Confirmation classes, my friend and me. The Reverend Maynard Smith was a wonderful man. To hear him read the lesson—he was just like a first-class actor."

The Reverend Hubert H.M. Bartleet

The Reverend Bartleet was Vicar of Malvern Priory from 1924 to 1947. His wife was a Foley, descendant of Lady Foley who owned the Manor of Malvern. So, the Priory living was hers to give to her husband.

"He was a little round, white-haired gentleman, with a very rosy face," said Joan Preece. "He was a very jolly little man and very well read," said George Morris.

The Revd. Bartleet used to write for the *Malvern Gazette* under the name of 'The Wyche Wizard'. He wrote this amusing poem, among many other poems and articles.

Lines to a Friend

Five Confirmation candidates have been with me today;
I've entered twice the Church's gate the services to say;
Books of Theology consumed
My morning hours with them entombed.

And now the Parish Magazine sits on my soul like lead;
Few contributions yet have been sent to the fountain-head;
Until the Magazine appears
The fountain issues nought but tears.

Hark! hark! the postman's knock I hear—a bill I see for me.
What's in this parcel? How I fear a savage writ to see!
Perhaps prospectus sent in hopes
That I'll invest in salt or soaps!

No! it's a poem, graceful, neat—the very thing to please;
Really, this kind contributor writes with uncommon ease,

Since he can furthermore enclose
A somewhat lengthy piece of prose!

He satirises all the Town. No-one escapes his whip.
Those smoking fellows 'A' and 'B', their wives (when tea they sip)
Who tear our characters to shreds,
And tell the tale whence scandal spreads.

Oh ripping! Here's a nasty one for fossil-hunting 'G'
And yet, by 'H', he seems to hit at book-collecting *me!*
Well! Well! He has not yet lit on
'Charles Lamb, a first edition'!

The Reverend Milne of Malvern Wells

Heather Talbot remembered him vividly. "At St. Peter's Church, Malvern Wells, the Reverend Milne was an exuberant man. His family services and encouragement of children was in advance of his time. It was not at all popular with the elderly ladies of the congregation. He loved children and was much liked at school, Sunday School, and Brownies, where he often popped in. Very refreshing he was!

The Reverend Milne would have the children out in front of the church to sing choruses, long before such things were normal. He had the inside walls of the church painted in bright colours. Each had a Biblical significance. It looked lovely when newly done."

The Work of a Sacristan

Helen Mooney was 95 in 1998, when she told me about her

long service as Sacristan, at St. Joseph's Roman Catholic church, Newtown Road.

"I've been Sacristan here for 51 years. I go in the church every day and prepare for every service. I did this even when I was teaching in the school here for 36 years. (She was Headmistress for 20 of those years). I prepare the vestments and the altar and put out the wine and wafers for Communion. After Mass, I clear it all up.

I've always done the washing of church vestments too. This morning, I've washed over two dozen purificators which are used with the chalice. I've washed the alb and the altar cloths. But someone else has washed the surplices."

For her 50 years' service as Sacristan, Helen Mooney has been awarded two quite rare Papal decorations. They are: BENI MERENTI meaning 'Well Merited', and PRO ECCLESIA PONTIFI meaning 'For the Roman Catholic church'. The Abbot of Douai presented these medals to Helen and she wears them on her white cassock in church.

The Mourning Bell

"The verger rang the mourning bell", said Minna Bowers. "It was a regular thing when a death was known, or when a funeral was about to take place. It was three times three for a man and three times two for a woman. Then a bell for every minute—a single toll, as was rung recently, at St. Matthias, for Princess Diana."

THE MAY QUEEN

Rose Revels and the May Queen ceremony at St. Matthias in the Link were held on the old Vicarage's vast lawn with its massive rhododendrons. The old Vicarage, now demolished, stood where Lyttelton Square houses are now in Church Road.

"The Rector chose the May Queen," said Madge Howard Davies. "And I made the dresses in the first place. I went to the Rag market in Birmingham and made all 20 dresses for less than £5. It was all nylon net. The little girl attendants' dresses were white. The little boys had white shirts, long blue trousers, red cummerbunds, and red bow ties.

When the May Queen retired at the end of the year, she made a little speech: 'I hope you will forget me not.' So, she became the Forget-me-not Queen in the following year. We had forget-me-nots in her basket and blue ribbons instead of pink ones. We had a fresh May Queen with new attendants, dressed accordingly. It was very difficult to get little boys to take part!

George Morris, Captain of the Bellringers, said he would find a telegraph pole for a maypole if I would find the coloured braids for it. You need very many yards of braid, of many colours. We tried shops in London, Birmingham, Gloucester, Bristol to get this amount of braid. Rings had to be sewn on all the braids.

But the teachers at Cromwell Road school still had to teach the children the maypole dances. They would rehearse in the playground, and one Headmaster would accompany them on his violin."

THE TRADITION OF BOY BISHOPS

In Mediaeval times, it was the custom at certain times of year, to reverse roles for a day. Those in authority were humbled and were replaced by an underling. A peasant became King for a day, while a King became a peasant. A choirboy (usually the

Head Chorister in a Cathedral) became Bishop. He was robed and mitred like a Bishop. He was expected to ascend into the pulpit and preach a short sermon, while the actual Bishop sat at his feet.

"Father Hartley started the tradition in the 1950's", said Madge Howard Davies. "We had a new and very beautiful costume made for the Boy Bishop, and he would accompany the May Queen and her attendants."

A great many events of a social nature, involving all age groups, centred around the church, in the days before television and computers.

"As well as teaching in Sunday School at St. Matthias, my husband and I produced pantomimes," Madge Howard Davies recalled. "They raised money for a car for a missionary in Africa. We did Peter Pan, Cinderella and Snow White and the Seven Dwarfs. This was in the late 1940's.

Materials were so short during and after the war, so I cut up all my white flannelette blankets, to make jackets and hoods for the Lost Boys of Never Never Land. For the beards of the seven dwarfs, I managed to get butter muslin from the chemist's. It was cheap and we fixed it on with elastic at the back. Then we sewed on tufts of cotton wool on their jackets to represent snow.

It was hard work getting all the costumes to fit. Mrs. Williams used to help 'cos she was a dressmaker. She was known as The Lady with the Lamp because she replenished the oil in the lamp in our Lady Chapel. Getting the children to rehearse was quite a job. But in those days, there were fewer distractions.

For Peter Pan, in 1949, there was scarlet fever about, and several children were absent from rehearsals. So, my daughter, Megan, had to take three parts, including Captain Hook. But Megan knew every move. My younger daughter, Lynn, was Tinker Bell."

Here is a report from the *Malvern Gazette* on 3rd January 1948 about St. Matthias children's pantomime, SNOW WHITE AND THE SEVEN DWARFS. Note the old-fashioned flowery, journalistic style! We were, of course, still rationed for food and clothes in 1948.

"The refreshing naivete and charm of their performance communicated much happiness to others. For just as the old year was dying, these clever youngsters transported a large audience straight to fairyland.

Soon came the woodland fairies and pixies and an enormous ghost. Perhaps he was the ghost of 1947, for he appeared to have suffered so much austerity that he must needs carry off two tiny pixies.

The Wardrobe Mistress, Mrs. Williams, must have had a fairy wand herself, to have secured such an amazing amount of pretty material for costumes."

CHURCH CLUBS AND PLAYS

In the 1940's and 1950's, before the universal appearance and enslavement of television and computers and the Internet, St. Matthias boasted several Clubs. There was the Youth Club, the Candle Club, and a good Dramatic Society.

"The church was at its best in those years," said Gwen Forster. "People from the Ascension church went automatically to the mother church, St. Matthias, for all special occasions. We were very united and there was a good spiritual influence then."

Gwen described the big historical Pageant performed at St. Matthias in 1947. "I was Wardrobe Mistress. I studied costume for three months before we started. We were still rationed then for clothing, but we asked people for curtains, sheets, bedspreads—and it came! It was amazing! A whole roll of blackout material turned up on the Vicarage porch one day. No one knows where it came from—to this day. It was very useful for the black garments of 'the monks of Pershore Abbey' in our pageant. Our church has links with Pershore Abbey in history.

There were about 250 people in the Pageant. The only costumes we hired were for the King Charles period, and soldiers' uniforms. All the rest we made ourselves. Different scenes were rehearsed separately by different groups.

To cap it all, Father Hartley said, 'I want a Victorian congregation for the last scene'. I said 'No!' and I sat down. I asked him to appeal from the pulpit for people's grandmothers' gowns. We received two trunk loads of Victorian crinoline costumes! Miss Evelyn Tait made all the bonnets.

The Misses Edwardes in the Link were the grand daughters of Lord and Lady Brougham, the people who gave their name to the brougham carriage. They gave us lovely Victorian crinolines worn by their mother. I sent these afterwards to Gloucester Museum. The Pageant was a great success. It was performed in the old Vicarage garden."

Gwen Forster, who is now in her 90's, produced several plays over the years. She told me: "I was asked to write and produce a Nativity play which brought in Bread and Wine. So, I wrote The House of Bread, which is the meaning of BETHLEHEM.

The Angel Gabriel takes a choirboy (played by Roger Dance) to see the Birth of Jesus in a stable. The climax of the play came when the two Archangels, Raphael, and Michael, appeared, standing on the High altar of the church. Below them were Mary, Joseph, and the newborn Babe. The priest held up the Sacrament of Bread and Wine.

All the congregation knelt down spontaneously at this point. I was pulling curtains and tears streamed down my face. 'How did she write it?' people asked. 'She prayed herself into it,' was the reply. Yes, I did. I was often on my knees, in the Lady Chapel.

We always had prayers before rehearsals. I was the Virgin Mary in another play. I had to meet and talk with the mother of Judas Iscariot, who was played by Ivy Dance."

But Gwen was versatile and could turn her hand to comedy too. "We performed '1066 and All That'. A huge number of people took part. We began with the Romans and ended up with the scene in India—Mad Dogs and Englishmen. I was the wife of the Common Man (played by Father Brown), and I carried my shopping bag."

CHURCH EMBROIDERY

St. Matthias Church has long been associated with beautiful vestments and altar frontals. "I first started with church embroidery in 1928," said Minna Bowers. "Miss Crystal, an Art mistress at Worcester Girls' Grammar School started the group here. Eventually, it was led by Miss Tait. She had been at the Royal School of Needlework.

We formed an Embroidery Guild, instructed by Miss Tait. Our group consisted of Joyce Anderson, Mary Jeavons, Gwen

Forster, Nadia Dunning and me, Minna Bowers. Because we were a Guild, we got our materials from the Royal School of Needlework.

First of all, it was repairing vestments. Then we made a lot of new vestments. For the church of the Ascension, we made a green frontal and green vestments, as a memorial to their choirmen and servers who had died in both world wars.

For St. Matthias we made a set of vestments in black and gold for Requiems, and the purple set used for Advent and Lent. There was a fine display of our embroidered vestments and altar frontals, enhanced by a Flower Festival, in St. Matthias church, in September 1995."

MALVERN PRIORY

A Malvern Chorister Remembers …

Brian Beale wrote these memoirs. "I was born at Walmer Lodge Hotel, Abbey Road, Malvern. My parents ran this hotel for 40 years.

When I was five, I was sent to join my sister, at Mowbray Collegiate School, until the age of eight. This building is now a Nursing Home in Victoria Road.

From 1921 to 1927, I was a pupil at the Lyttelton Grammar School, which was really a Choir School for Malvern Priory. I had to report to Dr. Hamand, the Organist and Choirmaster, in the Choir Room. I was given a sight-reading test from a Cathedral Psalm Book. After that, I had to sing scales up to top 'A'. Then I was asked to sing all the verses of 'There is a green hill far away', followed by the first and third verses of 'Lord, Thy Word Abideth'.

Dr. Hamand decided that I was good enough to be accepted. He told me to report for Choir practice on Mondays to Saturdays 9-9.45 a.m., and on Friday evenings 8-9 p.m. After a month, I was singing in the Choir for the Sunday service at 11 o'clock. For our uniform in school, we had to wear Eton coat, vest and trousers, a stiff round collar, black tie, and a Mortarboard with a blue tassel.

The first Friday, after choir practice, I was grabbed by some of the older boys and taken to the top of the steps opposite the Priory entrance door. Here, there was a tap on the grass. My head was held under the tap for a real soaking. It was the initiation for all new choristers—all in good humour, of course."

"I've sung in the Priory choir for 72 years now," said Jack Lewis to me, in 1997. "I was under Dr. Hamand, who was a pretty marvellous man. We boys had to get to the Priory on Friday evenings and back home to West Malvern on foot. No cars waiting to pick us up then!

When I was 16, Dr. Hamand said to me, 'What about trying a bit of alto?' So, I never left the choir. I just sat with the men. I sing alto still. It's rather a rare thing nowadays. But I can also manage bass. I shall be going on for a little while. I'm 81 now." (In 1997).

Dr. Hamand, the organist and choirmaster was a great man. He was organist at the Priory for 35 years. Dr. Hamand was an authority on old churches and stained glass. He was also a painter of considerable repute and had quite a few paintings in London galleries.

He had great respect from the boys. But he also conducted

an Oratorio Choir of 80 people in Malvern. He always had interesting things to say about birds—a real nature lover, he was. And, of course, he was a friend of Sir Edward Elgar and Sir Ivor Atkins."

In 1927, a new organ was installed in the Priory. It had been built by Rushworth and Dreaper of Liverpool. Dr. Louis Hamand had himself raised £6,000 for this new organ. In August 1998, the Canadian organist, Ashley Tidy, praised 'the clarity and sweetness of the organ pipes', after his recital on it.

Louis Hamand had an artist's eye for detail and for the beauty of nature and the landscape around Malvern. After all, he lived here for 35 years. I make no apology for including the following apt observations taken from his book *An Organist Remembers*, published in 1949:

"One day, the Priory Vicar asked a choirboy's opinion of me. The boy replied without any hesitation: 'Dr. Hamand is very strict; but he's always fair.'

My work took me over the hills to West Malvern to teach music in St. James's School. The route lay past St. Ann's Well. This walk was done in all weathers. In summer, it was delightful. In winter, it could be extremely difficult and dangerous. At that time, the postmen used to walk to West Malvern, carrying their loads over the hill. I have seen them reduced to crawling up on their hands and knees. Now the postmen *ride* nearly all of the long and difficult routes.

From the top of the Malvern Hills there is one of the fairest prospects to be seen in all of England. I have looked upon it some hundreds of times, in every variety of season, weather and time of day; under the serene beauty of a cloudless summer sky, or with heavy rainstorms scudding across the landscape. But it is the constantly changing scene, caused by sunshine and light clouds, chasing each other across the countryside, that is perhaps the most enchanting.

Our garden, at 'The Dingle', Christchurch Road, Malvern, is, rather surprisingly for a town garden, a veritable paradise for the bird-lover. A few moments ago, I caught sight of a white throat in a tree. We have an oak tree of great age and size. Moving up its trunk, we can often see from our windows the treecreeper, nuthatch, and green woodpecker with his bright red topknot and funny laughing cry.

Now and again, the railway station nearby, furnishes us with a strange music—the whir of wings, as flocks of homing-pigeons are released from their crates to start their homeward flight. Their circular movement gives a pleasant and musical effect of rhythm, casting a fleeting patch of shadow over the landscape.

It was a habit of mine to occupy myself during sermon-time in sketching the preacher, who from the organ-loft was admirably seen in profile. This did not deter me from listening to the discourse—rather, I think, the contrary. Beneath my finished drawing, I would scribble the sentence that happened to be spoken at the moment. By degrees, I acquired quite a portrait gallery of sketches.

It so happens that from the organ loft can be had one of the best views of the interior of the Priory. Many a time, before sitting down to play the organ, I have stood and gazed at the beauty of it all—always fresh, always a delight.

We held Christmas gatherings for the choir at our home. The men came for supper, the boys on another day for tea. My wife prepared an excellent repast of turkey, Christmas pudding and mince pies. The boys' tea, with Christmas crackers, was followed by 'fun and games', and prizes for the winners. The boys sang carols. These homely festivities were the means of bringing us all closer together and strengthening the bonds of friendship.

My old friend, Albert Sammons, the famous violinist, came and played the slow movement from Elgar's violin concerto in the Priory with organ accompaniment. As the dim light of a November afternoon gradually faded and he played in almost darkness, there was an added effect of mystery in the enchantment of his music.

During one season of the Malvern Festival in the 1930's, our seats happened to be immediately behind those of Sir Edward Elgar and Bernard Shaw, sitting together. They provided a fascinating study in silhouette.

During the Second World War, I found a new pursuit of absorbing interest. The absence of all street lighting gave a new and unexpected brilliance and beauty to the stars, especially when there was no moon. I was thrown into the company of a man with a first-rate knowledge of astronomy. I soon got to know some of the major constellations and planets, merely by standing in our own garden. Soon I began trying to get the choirboys to share it with me. Most of them did not even know the Great Bear or the Pole star. But some of the older boys proved to be quite good at picking out and remembering fresh stars and planets."

The Reverend William Fraser was Senior Curate at Malvern Priory from 1932-1936. He was responsible for visiting Malvern residents in all the roads south of Church Street. The other Curate was responsible for the area on the north side.

Now, aged 95, the Reverend Fraser still has in his possession the book in which he had to record all his Pastoral visits during that time.

One of the Malvern 'personalities' of those years was Mrs. Gripper of Abbey Road. She was tall and elegant and had a powerful presence. Apparently, Mr. Fraser was often bidden 'to take tea' at her 'At Homes'. He remembers, on one occasion, when he was passing round the cake stand to her guests, that Mrs. Gripper remarked, 'Poor Mr. Fraser, I don't believe he has had any tea at all!'

Doris Smith has a memory of Ascension Day in the 1920's and 1930's. "My parents owned and ran Aldwyn Tower Hotel, which is about 200 feet above the town of Great Malvern. We had a fine view of Malvern Priory. For many years, an Ascension Day service was held on the roof of the Priory tower at 9 a.m.

The guests at our hotel were told at dinner on the previous day that the Breakfast Bell would be rung on the following morning, at ten minutes to nine. This was so that guests could assemble on the balcony to see and hear the service sung by the choir and clergy.

The Ascension hymn, 'Hail the day that sees Him rise', sounded marvellous, ringing out on the clear morning air. It was followed by prayers for the day. Before descending, the choirboys would take off their surplices and wave them between the battlements to greet their friends in the churchyard below. A similar service is held at Pershore Abbey."

Elizabeth Guise Berrow told me of her visit to the Pope in Rome: "I had an English friend who spent his holidays in Rome when I was there. He said how much he would like to accompany me on an audience to see the Holy Father. I went to the British Consul to arrange it.

I had been Treasurer of Worcester Catholic History Society for some years, and I was staying with my Italian friends, the Pala family. They were very well known in the Vatican. So, there was no difficulty in arranging the visit—and for my friend too.

The following day, a Papal Messenger, attired in Papal uniform came to the Pala's house with an invitation. But we only had about two days' notice. I was the first person the Pope spoke to as he could talk to us privately. There were two other couples with us in this very big room.

I wore a long black dress and a black mantilla, which I always took with me when I went to Rome, as I often went to St. Peter's when in Rome. I have a photo of us both, standing in front of the Papal chair, after the ceremony."

Church Bells

We always associate going to church with church bells ringing. George Morris is a very experienced bellringer:

"When I was a boy, our house was in the Malvern Priory churchyard, as my father was Custos there. I very soon crept up the tower of the Priory. Tunes were coming out of the tower, and I was curious about the bells. At the top, were a couple of lads in the ringing chamber. They were 'chiming'. You can chime tunes on bells.

Very soon, I was hooked on bellringing. From the age of 15, I was ringing all weekends and at any other time. A band of ringers was started at the Priory. I joined them. Then I went to Claines to learn more, as *they* were a strong band. There were very few women and girls then, as bellringers.

Very few people would teach you. Much later on, as the Ringing Master of this district, I went to St. Matthias to instruct those ringers. I've been there permanently ever since. I met my wife there. We, at St. Matthias, were the first bellring-ers to make contact with Italian bellringers in 1984. We have made exchanges with them ever since.

The Veronese way of ringing resembles our English way. But they ring tunes, and we ring changes. St. Dunstan came from Italy to England. He may very well have brought with him the Veronese way of ringing—he and his monks. By 'Veronese' I mean the area between Lake Garda and Venice.

Our bellringers have taken part in Veronese competitions in Italy. We came ninth out of eleven. We have rung in Verona and Vicenza and in many other Italian churches.

My wife, Ruth, is good at the Italian system. So, there was a queue of Italian men bellringers wanting to ring with her, on five bells of a little church in the Italian mountains. As there are very few Italian women who ring, Ruth was quite a novelty!"

13 ~ Home and Family Life, Food and Drink

•••••••••••••••••

Before the invention of washing machines, vacuum cleaners, refrigerators and other such helpful modern 'necessities', life in the home was often hard work, especially for mothers of large families. Before the days of the Welfare State, families had to be resourceful, economical, and self-sacrificing.

Ethel Hall, who was born in 1890, told me about house-keeping in the 1890's: "My mother died when I was quite small. As I had three brothers older than me and two sisters, my father found a housekeeper to look after us. It was all hand labour in those days. There was a lot of washing to do. We girls wore pinafores all day, every day. A washer woman came every week to wash our clothes in a copper boiler and mangle them by hand."

"We were a family of twelve children", said Peter Treherne. "There would be 14 or 16 people in the house for tea on Sunday—a lot of work, preparing the meals. We all had our jobs, we children—like washing up. On Saturdays I helped my father on his big allotment."

"There were seven children in our family", Win Foster told me. "We were kept on £3 a week. But we had good clothes and good food, 'cos we had pigeons and rabbits and firewood—things that didn't cost much. We survived. We used to fetch milk from the farm in a can.

We were such a big family that I was always the one that had to stay in and darn the socks for everyone. There was always a job for us children to do for our parents. I had to bath one of the younger ones before going to bed."

Dorothy Jones remembered *her* Saturday morning jobs as a child. "We had to cut up pages of 'John Bull' magazine for the toilet. We cut each page into four pieces and put a piece of string through the corner. We wore black wool stockings. Those heels used to wear out into holes resembling 'potatoes'. One of your jobs for a Saturday morning was to 'mend the taters', as we used to say!"

Muriel Lanchester (who with her husband created the Lanchester Marionettes in Malvern) wanted a Housekeeper. Midge Tompkins applied, and Muriel gave her three tests: Clean a window. Clean a pair of shoes. Make a white sauce. Midge passed the tests and was appointed Housekeeper.

Mothers had to be strict. "Women would lean on the gate posts, gossiping in Upper Welland," said Margaret Davis. "Mother would never let us play in the road. We had to keep in our big garden. It was for our own good. Some of the boys were not too gentle."

OUTSIDE PRIVIES

In the 1920's, there were few home comforts in the villages. Reg Green recalled: "In Guarlford we had no piped water—only an old-fashioned pump, which served three cottages. Electricity had not yet arrived in the countryside. We depended on paraffin lamps and candles for illumination.

The cottage had no indoor sanitation. The 'privy' was down the garden, next to the pigsty. I had the job of emptying the bucket onto the garden, usually in the early morning when no one was around. I also cleaned out the pigsty."

Malvern town itself with its abundant springs seems to have installed flushing toilets much earlier than other towns nearby. In the early 1900's, an advertisement describes a certain Jim Tudge as a 'water closet installer'.

But in Pershore, even in 1931, we still had wooden seat and bucket privies, which were emptied each week by the nightsoil men. As a child, awakened by their scraping noises and muffled voices, I used to think they were gardeners working late! You avoided meeting their horse-drawn nightsoil cart because of the nauseating smell of the contents.

However, beyond elegant and hygienic Malvern, in the 1930's, and '40's and '50's, there were still outside earth closets in the surrounding villages.

Dorothy Jones, as a musical child, used to sing to herself in her grandmother's outside loo, at Callow End. You sang to keep up your spirits, especially on a dark night, and also to warn other people you were there.

Mary Wells had an auntie who lived at 19 Greenfield Road, Malvern Link, in the 1930's. The one-hole privy in the garden there, had an immense board of white deal, one yard long, and scrubbed frequently, using bleach.

An amusing privy anecdote is related by Mary Wells: "Seventy years ago, my grandmother lived at 42 Redland Road and had an outside loo. Whenever her sister-in-law, Jessica, came to visit via the front door my grandmother would gather up a candle and the evening newspaper and disappear through the back door. So, my grandfather was left alone to entertain his sister Jessica. The reason for this was that grandmother could not stand Jessica's airs and graces. Jessica was currently

Housekeeper to 'Uncle David' Davis, of the BBC radio Children's Hour. He lived at The Oaks, Graham Road, Malvern. Because Jessica mixed with the gentry, she would give everyone homilies on how to behave, wearing her royal blue Housekeeper's dress and starched white apron.

And she would talk of 'putting my cakes in the *h*oven'. As my grandmother was an excellent cook, who made superb sponge cakes with her own hens' fresh eggs (and her sponge cakes always rose to six inches), she did not need Jessica's sermons.

So, grandmother preferred to sit outside in the cold, on the loo, with a candle stuck on the wall, reading the evening newspaper. Outside loos were thus quite often a haven of escape.

Nevertheless, Grandmother would be quite pleased to hear her husband call out, after an appropriate interval, 'It's alright. She's gone now, Millie!'"

WATER AND POWER

"For a bath", said Alma Longstaff, "we had to boil the water in a copper. Only *cold* water taps were on our bath. Us three girls had to share the bath water—all in the tub together."

"Houses in Church Road, Malvern Link, were lit by gas mantles in the 1930's", recalled Dorothy Jones.

Mary Wells recollected: "We had a Triplex grate—very popular then, in the 1930's. I had to clean the flues out every Saturday morning—my day off from school. All the soot would come out. Otherwise, the oven wouldn't get hot.

Electricity was a tremendous upheaval for us. My mother had complained about getting the saucepans dirty if you put them on top of the fire. It would take you ages to clean them. So, it was so nice to have *clean* electricity!

I remember the first day we had an electric cooker, in 1956. We were frightened to use it. It was quite a big adventure. I said I would do Welsh Rarebit on the top, and we could try the oven tomorrow. At the M.E.B. we had cookery demonstrations. I went to every single one of those, so that I could be conversant with our Jackson electric cooker. I learnt how to make Yorkshire puddings there, for which I've been famous for the last 40 years!"

FOOD

"My mother was hard put to feed us eight children in 1914, when we lived in Upton-on-Severn", recalled Austin Hartwright. "But Lady Tennant would give us beef dripping. My mother was her dressmaker. And a local shop gave us good bacon dripping.

Breakfast would often be a hunk of bread, soaked in tea, with brown sugar on top. For mid-day at school, mother would give us bread, and two pence each to buy a good hunk of corned beef or cheese. Very occasionally, there would be bread pudding made with suet.

Yet we always had plenty of energy, and we were happy."

Charles Smith remembered dripping on toast as a boy. "That was my favourite—making toast by the coal fire, on a fork, 'cos toast made by the fire is **much** nicer than done by gas. There's no comparison."

"Eggs were put down in ising glass to preserve them during the winter, when I was a boy", recalled Derek Davidson. "There were no fridges then, so, in cool larders, we put net covers on jugs of milk, to keep the flies out."

Freda Morris had tasty memories of elvers. "They get them

in Gloucester. They only come into the Severn. The salmon come to lay their eggs. The elvers (very young salmon) are like little worms, pure white. You have to boil them first. They go a greyish colour. You fry them in fat and salt. They're beautiful—makes my mouth water! I got to know elvers in the Forest of Dean, not far from Cinderford, where my mother was born and brought up, on a farm."

Ethel Hall was brought up on a farm also. She was 108 in December 1998. She recollected: "On our farm in Somerset, the milk was of good quality. We had plenty of butter and eggs. We made cheese too. We always had homemade cakes. We were brought up on boiled puddings—roly-poly's with sultanas, or plain puddings with golden syrup or jam. And there was always CREAM!

We had cream with everything! When my brothers had second helpings of the meat and vegetables and if the gravy was short, they would pour cream on their meat and vegetables! Our doctor couldn't believe it. But our housekeeper said, 'Try it doctor! You'll like it!' The cream was from the top of our rich milk."

Helen Cutler's aunt was an excellent cook. Helen recalled: "I lived with my aunt, who kept an apartment house. She had gone as a young woman to a Cookery school in Gloucester. But she started her career in Blenheim Palace, 'cos she was brought up in Oxfordshire. You worked in big houses then.

I've never had such good food as I had at my aunt's, as a child. I loved curry. Nobody had heard of it then. (Perhaps her aunt had cooked with it at Blenheim). Every November we had jugged hare (another gentleman's dish). It was all very proper! For Christmas it was chicken. We had never heard of turkey then."

Elsie Jennings related: "Next door they kept a pig. They used to make lovely lard flavoured with rosemary. And they gave my mum chitlings from the pig. But they made such a fuss of their last pig, that they couldn't eat it. It became a friend!"

"Everybody at the Wyche had pigs", said 'Divvy' Davis. "You had to pass the pig to go to the outside toilet. There was one toilet—a bucket—between two houses. You could hear each other, of course. As a boy I loved this pig. I used to pull something out of the garden—a carrot—for him. He always wanted a snippet.

Anyway, they killed this pig. And neighbours would watch. They grabbed this pig, poor devil, and they put him on a bench. They tied 'im down. And the pig knew—and didn't he squeal! They cut 'is throat, like that. And the **children** were watching! It was the excitement, you see. And the next time 'e come to kill that pig my mother saw to it *I* was not about."

Fowls sometimes became household pets. Elsie Jennings remembered: "We kept fowls. One of them followed my Mum everywhere and into the house. But my Mum would never eat it."

Ellen Hymas recalled: "My mother was very good at making something out of nothing. She would make a broth out of a breast of lamb. And I remember her good meat puddings when she lined the pudding basin with suet."

"When I was a child," related Ellen Hymas, "we never ate white bread. That was for the gentry. My grandfather grew corn at his farm in Berrow, and he took it to a mill to be ground into flour. My grandmother made brown bread, which always had a heavy 'bottom'.

My mother and her sister took bread to eat in the school playground, at dinner time. But they did not like the other children to see them eating such coarse brown bread. It was considered inferior to white bread in those days."

PUDDINGS

Many people enthused about their mothers' homemade puddings. 'Divvy' Davis recalled 'constant rice puddings', while Helen Mooney remembered 'plenty of apple pies and jam tarts'.

"We were given heavy Spotted Dick, made in a cloth and put into a saucepan," said Charles Smith. "You don't see that today."

"Our rice puddings were cooked by my mother in the black-leaded oven," said Margaret Hands. "And I used to hate rhubarb tarts! The thought of them sets my teeth on edge, even now! But on Sundays, we had a tin of pineapple. *That* was a treat!"

"Puddings filled you up", explained Alma Longstaff. "We grew our own apples for our large family. There were strawberry beds on my father's allotment. I remember our mother's treacle tarts. And my father's loganberries with Carnation milk."

Jam making and preserving fruit was considered essential by housewives, up to the 1960's—especially in wartime. "On Cowleigh Bank we had a damson tree," said Helen Mooney. "We all gave up sugar in our tea so that we could make damson jam. They were pretty grim days in the First World War."

Ethel Hall, aged 108, had happier memories: "From our Somerset farm, we went to Cheddar every summer for straw-berries—the large ones for dessert. At the end of the season, we bought the small ones for making jam. We made a lot of jam and pickles. Our Somerset orchards had cider apples and 'keepers' like Blenheim Orange and Beauty of Bath."

Gordon Griffith had vivid memories of his mother's cooking. "She was well known in West Malvern for her culinary skills. Her marvellous pastry, I remember well. At Whist Drives over the road, she used to supply the coffee. She would filter it, once or twice, just like wine."

It was her *father's* cooking that Winnie Barnes recalled: "Mother never did the cooking because she was delicate and had a patch on her lung. She was in the Sanatorium for five months. I was three then. Dad made a good stew and dumplings, but he was no good at pastry. We had Spotted Dicks for puddings, and he made lovely cakes. Dad had to do the washing and ironing when he came home from work while mother was ill.

When mother was well, she never went out to work—not even to a hop field. She never even did the shopping or housework! We waited on her and Dad pampered her. She lived till she was 96, 'cos she was well looked after."

FOOD AT CHRISTMAS

"It was open house at Christmas", said Ivy Pitt, "in my mother's young days. She told me you would share your Christmas meal with any visitors who called. Even if it was the doctor who called, he was invited to sit down and have a meal. It was beef, pork, or cockerel then. No turkeys. A cockerel was juicier than a turkey."

Freda Morris, now in her late 70's, is still very busy during the Christmas season. For her seven children and numerous grandchildren, she bakes Christmas cakes as Christmas presents.

She told me: "I usually make about 14 Christmas cakes.

I start in October. The longer you keep them, the better they are. I make loads of mince pies. That's my children's Christmas present—a Christmas cake, three dozen mince pies and about 5 or 6 apple tarts for each of my sons and daughters.

I store them in a little room upstairs. I don't make the mince pies and apple tarts until the day before they visit me. And as they come home at separate times, I don't have them all to do at once. I get up at 5 a.m. to do all this." What a wonderful mother is Freda! Still reflecting the self-sacrifice of past generations of mothers!

"The allotments holders all had a pigsty," said Francis Bird. "To get the pigs as fat as they were, the pig owners used to walk as far as Blackmore, to the American camp, during the war. Or they went to HMS Duke, to the cookhouse. Or to Wood Farm or Merebrook, which was the SAS camp. This was to get their pigswill. They collected it in dustbins on wheels.

They would build a little Furness. And find an old copper, used for washing. They would boil their pigswill in this.

In those days, you could dry out your potatoes on your garden, and leave them there for three or four days. And they'd still be there. Nobody would think of helping themselves. The same with the fruit on the trees.

Miss Holland had a big orchard at the top of Knoll Lane. It stretched right down to what is now Bredon Grove. Her nephew, Ken Wiggins, the choirmaster, picked her apples for her.

She used to wrap them individually in newspaper. They were all on trays in her shed. There were Blenheims and Russets—apples that would keep over Christmas. You could buy your apples off her. They were beautiful."

HOME MADE WINE

"My mother made homemade wine", said Frank Burston. "But she wouldn't let anyone touch it till it was two years of age. She made dandelion, parsley, elderberry, and elderflower. You can make wine with oak leaves, and wine from wheat."

Joan Preece told me: "I made wine from blackberries, damsons and rose hips, and elderberry champagne. It was a lot of work! When bottled, you had to watch it—or out would pop the corks! You had to tighten them up a little every day."

Home-made wine was frequently offered to visitors to one's home. Joy Van Daesdonk had happy memories of this. "The first time I took my husband-to-be to visit my relatives in Tenbury Wells, we went on the train for the day. We came home on the last train back to Malvern Wells. By the time we'd got round all the family in Tenbury Wells, and they had all given us homemade wines, we were pretty well … 'tanked up', 'cos you had to be polite. On the train home we were carrying a dozen new laid eggs, in a punnet. Walking back from the Wells station with the eggs, we rolled home, very happy!"

"My mother used to make Herb Beer", recalled Meriel Hodgetts. "She made it out of dandelions, nettles, and goosegrass. Mother boiled the herbs and added yeast. It made a very nice drink. As children, we drank nothing else. And we all had beautiful skins!"

Ellen Hymas told me: "My mother made Ginger Beer. She put a ginger beer plant in a jar, with sugar and water. It would work up and down to make a good drink of ginger beer."

FAMILY AMUSEMENTS

Mary Wells declared, thoughtfully, "Smells and sounds can recapture the exact atmosphere of past experiences. My parents were ballroom dancers and had lots of 78 records of 1930's songs. Now, when I hear 'Tip Toe thro' the Tulips', 'Painting the Clouds with Sunshine' and 'No, No, Nanette', I am back as a 12-year-old girl in our kitchen where Mother and Father are practising dancing to the gramophone music."

In the 1930's, people were content with simple pleasures. "As children, we often listened to the wireless", said Dorothy Jones. "On Children's Hour, Uncle Mac and Uncle David would say 'Hello Children Everywhere'. There were lots of programmes we liked—Monday Night at Eight, Band Waggon, In Town Tonight, The Man in Black ... That was long before the days of television. And at 9.30 p.m. we used to have our cocoa and go to bed."

Helen Mooney's memories of childhood go back to the early 1900's. She was 95 in 1998. She recalled: "After church on a Sunday evening, in summer, the whole family would go for a walk in the countryside. We went past Pale Manor, towards Leigh Sinton and across the fields, past the Isolation Hospital.

You can come out by the edge of the brook on the Storridge Road where the county boundary was. It was a great thing to stand with one foot in Worcestershire and one foot in Herefordshire. That was the standard summertime walk for the family."

HOLIDAYS

Holidays away from home in the 1930's were in no way exotic

or "going abroad". "My father was a railwayman," said Minna Bowers, "so we often travelled by rail to see a city, for the day, or to the seaside, to Barry Island or Porthcawl."

Jim Tudge recollected: "As my father worked on the railway, he was allowed twice a year tickets for the whole family to travel by rail. So, although poor, we always went away for a summer holiday, usually to Weston-Super-Mare.

And it was a lovely feeling when the steam train gave its first 'Poof!' to think we were on holiday! We would set off from Malvern Wells station then. A pity that station has gone!"

"We had an aunt in Swanage as kept the boarding house", said Joan Preece. "Every year we went to Swanage on the old Midland Railway. To Upton, then Ripple (change at Ripple). On to the Cheltenham train. Change at Wareham. It was all changes! We always went for the first two weeks in September. So, I used to have an extra week's holiday from school—which pleased me! But my auntie's house was bombed out in the war."

Gordon Griffith remembered countryside holidays in Bosbury, Herefordshire. "My mother used to take me and my younger brother, on push bikes to Bosbury, for a week or a fortnight in summer. She knew the people who lived in the gardener's cottage. We would be aged only 5, 6, or 7 then.

It was half-a-mile down to the village. At the cottage, the entertainment was to sit outside on a stool by the chicken runs, and keep quiet, and watch the *rats* come out!"

CLOTHES & UNDERCLOTHES

Clothes were often made at home by skilful mothers who knew how to sew and knit. "My Mum used to make most of our clothes", said Dorothy Jones proudly. "The patience my Mum

197

had! It was winceyette for our nighties, corduroy, and velveteen for our winter dress. She made our coats too. We used to hear her machining when we were in bed—a wonderful mother! Once we had got ready for the winter term, we'd buy our macs and sou'westers at the Co-op. And our wellingtons too."

Minna Bowers had a similar memory. "Until my mid-teens, I never wore a bought dress. It was all made by my mother. She used to make my brothers' suits as well. And she made underclothes. I've still got upstairs a nightie she made for me when I was a baby. It has tiny tucks around the bottom and tucks around the yoke and little bits of lace everywhere."

Underclothes provide an interesting history in themselves. Patricia Egerton, of Brays' Lingerie Department has managed a lingerie shop for many years and has great experience of foundation garments. She said, "I remember the lace-up and boned corsets of the 1930's. There is a softer feel now to lingerie. It is prettier, with lace trimmings."

The whalebones of Victorian corsets gave way to rustless steel in the 1890's, then to spiral steel bones from 1905. In 1922, many corsets had elastic inserts, and later on, elastic panels in front. The zip fastener and the 'roll on' arrived.

Warner Bros. launched the Lastex two-way stretch in 1931. This solved the problem of 'riding up'. Berlei arrived from Australia. Corset fitters visited customers in their own homes to measure them for Spirella corsets. The control brief is still very important in the Berlei corset market, for 'There can be no fashion without foundation'.

Patricia Egerton commented: "About bras—the Victorian 'binder' of ladies' bosoms, gave way to the Liberty bodices of the 1920's and then to brassieres or 'bras'. Suspenders were made redundant when tights took over."

One local titled lady, who was a little on the plump side, used to buy her clothes in Worcester at a size **smaller** than her actual size. This was quite deliberate on her part.

"And she left me with her newly bought outfits, for me to alter to fit her," added her dressmaker. "I had to take out the seams and sew them up again. And I often wondered whether, at her dinner parties, the seams ever 'popped'!"

Freda Morris recalled: "Malvern people went to Worcester to shop in the 1920's and '30's. It was the highlight of the week, going to Worcester and back by train. It cost sixpence return. Worcester had a market where you could buy loads of things. I bought my first evening dress there, on the market. It cost four shillings and eleven pence. It was a cerise colour in a satin material. It lasted for years. And my younger sisters used to dress up in it afterwards."

MATCH-MAKING

Ethel Hall, who was born in 1890, described matchmaking in Somerset, in the years 1910 to 1914. "Two or three young men came to see me. But I didn't fancy them. I was picking and choosing. I met my husband through his brother being in the church choir and **my** brothers knew **him**. I married at the age of 24. My husband was 30.

He was a butcher and had a good business—a shop, in Glastonbury. But he was a drinker and never saved money. After Somerset, we went to Essex. After he died, I re-married. I had three daughters and one son. Only one of my daughters and my son are living now."

FAMILY MUSIC

Long before television, computers, and the Internet were invented, families made their own music and entertainment. "Dad used to make us all sing around the piano—all seven of us children," said Dorothy Jones. "He would sing 'Oft in the stilly night', and 'Come into the garden, Maud'. Mum would be sewing. Happy days!"

Mary Wells had happy memories of musical evenings at home. "My father played the piano, at home, after a hard day's work. My mother sang all the old Victorian ballads. Our musical evenings were quite normal. So, I knew the words of all the old songs, and we had lots of hymns too.

I can hear my mother singing beautifully 'I dreamt that I dwelt in marble halls' and 'I know that my Redeemer liveth'. I never felt in the least deprived. If it was raining, and I could not go out on my bicycle, and there was always our musical evenings to look forward to."

LOOKING BACK

Let Jean Jones of Mathon conclude this chapter, with these wise and thoughtful words: "To write down our individual life story and read it in our twilight years—what memories and nostalgia it would evoke! What self-satisfaction or regrets would be revealed!

Writing is a powerful tool of expression. LIFE is like a BOOK. Each page is perhaps a new day. Each chapter is a new beginning—or even an ending."

POPULAR SONGS

I have always been acutely aware that a popular song can conjure up for each one of us the unique atmosphere of a particular occasion or era. Here are the titles of songs of the 1920's and '30's, harvested at random from my memory:

Tiptoe through the Tulips

The Wedding of the Painted Doll

The Broadway Melody

The Destiny Waltz

Have you Ever seen a Dream Walking?

Lazy Bones

You Must Say Yes to Mr. Brown

Everything's in rhythm with My heart

Dancing on the Ceiling

In Your Easter Bonnet

Love is the Sweetest Thing

Night and Day

I'm in the Mood for Love

My Heart Stood Still

What'll I Do?

Nice Work if You Can Get It

On the Good Ship Lollipop

Animal Crackers in My Soup

I Told Every Little Star

Miss Otis Regrets

Don't Forget, Dinner at Eight

Cherry Blossom Lane

September in the Rain

Room 504

There's a Small Hotel

The Love Bug

Smoke Gets in Your Eyes

These Foolish Things

Love Walked Right In

The Way You Look Tonight

Dancing Cheek to Cheek

Deep Purple

All the Things You Are

Waltzing in the Clouds

It's Foolish but it's Fun

On the Isle of Capri

A Nightingale sang in Berkeley Square

14 ~ We Coped with Illness, the Poor and the Needy

Long before the 'safety net' of the Welfare State came into existence, people put their trust in old and simple remedies to combat illness.

Poor people who could not afford to call in the doctor and pay him half-a-crown or a guinea (£1 and one shilling) went to the local chemist or pharmacist. He was often known as "better than a doctor". Some of his poorest customers would have to pay for his medicines in *kind*. They would bring him produce from their allotments or eggs from the farms.

DOCTORS

"Dr. Shakespeare in West Malvern was lovely!" exclaimed Mary Tudge. "He was a descendant of William Shakespeare. His son, Nicholas, writes in newspapers and books. His widow lives up here still. She must be nearly 100."

"Dr. Shakespeare was a marvellous man," added Jim Tudge. "On a cold day, one of our painters was waiting for the bus and Dr. Shakespeare pulled up in his car. The doctor said, 'You never ought to be waiting in the cold.' He took off his coat and gave it to this man. He was a generous man and very highly thought of. He was a good poet in his own right. Whenever

I was ill in bed, he would give me a classic book to read. One day, he arrived with an inscribed book of his own poems. He was very proud of being a descendant of William Shakespeare."

Francis Bird recalled two doctors in the Poolbrook and Barnards Green area. "Before the second world war, we had two doctors, Dr. Newton and Dr. Smythe. They were at Lodiswell, the surgery opposite Christchurch. Poolbrook people had no doctors closer than that. Dr. Newton used to wear spats over his shoes. He was super. Our chemist in Barnards Green, was Mr. Lamb, where the pet shop is now."

BABIES

Ellen Hymas had a hair-raising memory to relate: "When I was carrying my eldest daughter before she was born, I had to visit Nurse Brown at the Wyche, and I walked up there from Barnards Green, where I lived. It was bitterly cold. The trees were frozen that hard, the branches were cracking. It was in 1940, that very bad winter. I was slipping and sliding all the way. When I got there, the Nurse wasn't there! On the way back home I had the toothache, so I went into Woolworth's, and I bought some peppermints to keep me warm. I had Nurse Wiggins in Pickersleigh Road after that. *She* was my midwife. Dr. Scott came for the birth. I had all my children born at home. Dr. Meikle charged half-a-crown a visit and five shillings for any treatment."

Nadia Mary Dunning tells this amazing story of The Miracle Baby of Malvern Link: "In the 1920's, Dr. Meikle, a good old family doctor, brought into the world a premature baby girl, who weighed only 2 pounds three ounces at birth. That was ME! There were no incubators then or breathing apparatus in hospitals. So, Dr. Meikle said to my father, 'Go and find the biggest laundry basket you can. Line it with blankets and cotton wool.' *That* was to be the baby's incubator!"

Nadia continued: "I was kept at home in a warm place and fed every two hours on Nestle's milk with an Apostle spoon. Very slowly I gained weight, they told me. 'At least the wee one is not slipping back!' commented the good doctor. I was christened at home on the day I was born by Father Day of St. Matthias church. My father had seen the name Nadia in a book he was reading."

Nadia is still with us, now in her 70's, and is a regular worshipper at St. Matthias. "I must have been *strong!*" is her apt comment.

PHARMACISTS

There was praise too for the pharmacists of those days. Mary Tudge recalled: "We had a lovely chemist in West Malvern, called Mr. Bissett. Christopher, our eldest son, was always being ill with his chest. We were given the first lot of M. and B. tablets for him, and they did wonders. Our chemist was as good as a doctor. I remember the first television I ever saw was in Mr. Bissett's house. I had gone into the shop, and I *had* to see it. It was marvellous!"

Ivy Pitt remembered another well-liked chemist in West Malvern. "Mr. Cope was a wonderful old man. He was very tall and very thin. His lady was very thin as well. She would only eat raw food—a vegetarian. Mr. Cope was better than a doctor. He would help you. In those days you had to pay for a doctor."

Mary Tudge described Mr. Cope too: "He was a sweet little old man. He looked like something out of Dickens. It was a really old-fashioned shop, with all those glass jars around. But he wouldn't sell baby food. 'Mothers should feed their own babies', he said."

"We paid sixpence a week into the Hospital Fund", said Joy Van Daesdonk, who lived in Malvern Wells. "This continued until the 1948 National Health Scheme."

Joy told me about the Malvern Wells Dispensary Fund. "It had begun in Victorian times. My mother used to run that. She collected at the schools in Malvern Wells and the Wyche, once a month. You paid one or two shillings per household. That entitled you to your doctor for a very reduced sum, or for nothing."

SPECIAL HOSPITALS

People remember Fever and Isolation Hospitals—one at Welland and one at Half Key. Lots of families had at least one member with tuberculosis. They had to be isolated in a hut at the bottom of the garden or go to a Sanatorium.

Olive Goldsmith has vivid memories of having Scarlet Fever, as a little girl, aged four. "I was in the Isolation Hospital for nearly two months. My long dark ringlets were cut off and my hair grew straight afterwards. I had to have a bath in disinfectant. My mother had to hang a sheet soaked in disinfectant over the door and fumigate the bed and curtains.

I was put in an adults' ward in a very big cot. The women patients there were told to keep an eye on me. When I woke up, all eyes were on me. One lady in hospital wrote to my mother, because she was so concerned about me. You see, my mother was not allowed to visit me at all during all those weeks in hospital because of infection.

I was given a very heavy book to read. It was "Fatty 'Arbuckle", about a boy who was very fat and always eating. I put it aside! And when I went home, the doll I had taken with me had to be left behind in hospital!"

ST. CUTHBERT'S HOSPITAL

Wendy Grounds retains some hair-raising memories of her time as a nurse at St. Cuthbert's: "The Preliminary Training School for Nurses was where Baxhill Nursery School is now, in Worcester Road, Malvern Link. This was all part of St. Cuthbert's Hospital. Nurses did their preliminary training for 10 weeks. The full training in Birmingham Children's Hospital was for three years.

While training in Birmingham, nurses often did a spell at St. Cuthbert's. Here were children recovering from burns, T.B. cases, asthmatics, weak hearts, and so on. They were often at St. Cuthbert's for six months. There were beautiful gardens, where the children could play. Those well enough would attend the hospital school. Their parents were allowed to visit them once a fortnight. They would come out on the 144 Midland Red bus, which ran from Birmingham to Malvern every twenty minutes, and would stay with their children for a couple of hours.

I did a spell of night duty there. The night nurse slept in the top room of the Training School. My memory is of a cold room, over-run with mice. I was in charge of the children from 8 p.m. to 8 a.m. They slept in a large open-air ward, where the floor-to-ceiling windows were never closed. The Matron had locked her office so there was no telephone.

One night, during my three months' spell of night duty, a soldier got in. He was crouched under one of the children's beds. What his intentions were, I couldn't imagine. But when I shouted authoritatively at him, he ran out through the windows and up the Worcester Road.

Another time, men were stealing the coal from the cellar. Shortly after the war, fuel was in short supply, so I was forced to take action. I opened the cellar door, and shouted to them to leave some coal, as sick children needed the heating. They dropped their shovels and made a hasty retreat. No doubt they thought I was a phantom. My white apron would be all that was visible on top of the dark steps!"

"I taught in St. Cuthbert's Hospital School in Malvern Link," said Dorothy Pembridge. "It was on the Worcester Road, opposite the Common where Morgan Court now stands. It was a hospital for T.B. cases and an annexe of the Birmingham Children's Hospital.

We tried to get the children on the right Reading Schemes. Some of them stayed for a year, 'cos they were long-term cases. We had them up to 16 years of age. I played the piano for the songs, and we had a percussion band. The very young children had sand and water play. There was a nice garden and what I called The Magic Wood with trees which they could climb."

THE OPEN AIR SCHOOL, WEST MALVERN

Fifty years ago, Gary Taylor came as a boy to the Open Air School in West Malvern, to improve his health. This School had opened in 1914.

"Miss Severn Burrow, a County Councillor, planned the Open Air School," said Doris Smith. "It was created for children from Birmingham, who needed fresh air and good food. She used to call it Youngsters' Mount."

Gary Taylor recalled: "The doctor at my school clinic, in Lye, by Stourbridge, had recommended this course of fresh air treatment to my mother. It was just after the war, and, like several other children in my district, I was under-nourished. Other children were there because of their asthma, or bronchitis, or heart conditions.

Our dormitories had wooden shutters, which were open all day and all night. They would only be closed in heavy rain or snow. There were red blankets and waterproofs on our beds. Our classroom windows were always open. We did a lot of outside activities."

CHILDREN IN HOSPITAL

In 1932, my sister Avril, aged 3, and myself aged 8, were taken to Worcester Royal Infirmary to have our tonsils and adenoids removed on the advice of our family doctor in Pershore. This was a common operation in those days.

We were both in the Children's Ward—Bonaker Ward—which was austere. The nurses were formal. The Matron wore a starched white head-dress. Nothing was explained to children in those days. I did not at first understand the Nurse's questions about 'Number One and Number Two' (my bladder and bowel movements).

In the frightening operation room, I remember struggling under the unexpected ether mask. I can still smell it! Masked-faced attendants had to hold my stockinged legs down. I awoke with a very sore throat and swallowed a drink with difficulty.

There was nothing else but books to occupy us as we lay in bed. We watched the nurses on their rounds but had to stay in bed. Our mother was not allowed to visit us during our ten days in hospital. The policy everywhere then was, 'No visitors, because children would become upset. Parents would unsettle young patients.' So, it was a pleasant surprise for me, one morning, to receive a parcel of marigolds wrapped in damp newspaper from Mrs. Holland Martin of Overbury Court. My parents had lived in Overbury for nine years. I can still smell those welcome marigolds! Alas! my marigolds were at once whisked away by a starchy nurse and thrust into a vase on a distant table. I was near to tears.

Bedtime was 7 p.m. in that Ward. The Night Nurse kindly played the same records of popular songs, each evening, to send us to sleep. I can still hear the syrupy words and music of a current hit, 'Goodnight Sweetheart, see you in the morning'. It was meant to console us, but it only made me feel more apprehensive and sad at being 'imprisoned' and far from home.

1918 INFLUENZA EPIDEMIC

40 million people worldwide died in this horrendous epidemic. Many lives were claimed in the Malvern area and in other parts of Worcestershire. Some people blamed it on the return of soldiers from the war front in France but there is no evidence to support this theory. No-one ever knew the cause or the remedy. People aged 20 to 40 were the worst afflicted.

Here are some grim extracts from the County Medical Records for 1918:

> **The Chief Medical Officer states:** Influenza is not a 'Notifiable Disease', but as is well known, it was extraordinarily prevalent and very fatal in the County in 1918. 995 deaths were registered as due to Influenza. The average annual deaths from Influenza during the 3 previous years was 68.

Owing to the Doctors being overworked when Influenza was epidemic, no local pathological examinations were able to be made; nor were any bacteriological investigations practicable. There was no evidence throwing light on the means of introduction of the disease. No provision could be made for the removal of patients to the Isolation Hospital because no beds were available. Fewer Nurses were available, owing to the large number of cases.

It would have been impracticable to carry out disinfection at all the houses where Influenza occurred: even if those had been known, which they were not. Consequently, it was not attempted.

Heather Talbot, who was born in Malvern Wells, told me how her mother's whole life was affected by the 1918 'flu epidemic: "My mother, Eva George, was born in 1913 in Welland. As a child of 5, she lost both parents and her maternal grandfather in the course of a week during the 'flu epidemic of 1918. She was sent to live with her Grandfather and Granny George at Malvern Wells and was brought up by them. She left school at 14 to work in Holbrooks' the grocers and attended evening classes in shorthand and typing at Malvern Technical College. All her life she read books and she encouraged us from an early age to go to the library.

My mother was very hard-working. She had always walked everywhere in the Wells. When she worked at the shop, she walked home and back at lunchtime, especially to see her Granny. Her closest childhood friend told me that on my mother's wedding day, the bride had still fetched the coal in and cared for her Granny before going to church. My mother never felt sorry for herself in spite of her tragic early life."

GENERAL HOSPITALS IN MALVERN

The Cottage Hospital in Hospital Bank, Newtown, became too small. So, the present General (now Community) Hospital in Lansdowne Crescent was built and completed in 1911.

Disney Reynolds recollected: "In the first world war, we used to help at the Cottage Hospital in Hospital Bank. The first lot of soldiers had arrived there—the wounded from the battle front in France. We lads used to clean their boots!"

An interesting mention of Malvern's brand-new Hospital in Lansdowne Crescent occurs in a school magazine. Ivydene Hall, in Albert Road North, had been opened in 1893, as the embryo Malvern Girls' College.

In Ivydene's Coronation Number for the Summer Term of 1911 (the Coronation of King George V) the following items occur:

> *"The Ivydene cot was donated to the new Malvern Hospital, opened by Countess Beauchamp on Monday 29th May. On Pound Day, 107 Ivydenites wound their way to the Hospital with gifts and were shown 'our own cot'."*

Today, just inside the main door of Malvern's Hospital, the original drinking fountain with the green tiles is still to be seen.

The Manager, Terry Brickley, said in 1998, "Our patients must have quality and dignity. I want our treatment of them to include a spiritual side." With this positive attitude, it is no wonder that Malvern Community Hospital now receives the most 'Thank You' letters of all the hospitals in Worcestershire!

THE POOR OF MALVERN

Wendy Grounds of Malvern has researched extensively the history of this subject. Here are some of her discoveries, which she has kindly permitted me to quote:

"All through the ages, it has been a struggle to care for the needy of the parish and Malvern was no exception. Various local Charities were created to give out coal, blankets, and bread to the poor people of Malvern.

In the late 18th Century, a Poor House was built on the Worcester Road in Malvern Link. This pleasant house, now privately owned and called 'Beechlawn', had the facilities to employ able-bodied poor people as flax spinners. It thus became the Parish Workhouse. But the wandering poor of other parishes were not encouraged.

In this Workhouse, the paupers would have regular meals and a roof over their heads. Apart from the infirm and old, there were numbers of people who, through sickness or bad luck had no work. Failed harvests, changes in agriculture, accidents, cessation of wars—all these could throw people into penury.

A Master was appointed to run the Workhouse and he was paid a yearly salary. People in the parish who owned property or land paid a Poor Rate. In 1834, a New Poor Law Act came about. Parishes were to be grouped into Unions of Parishes. Upton-on-Severn was considered the right place to build the Union Workhouse for all the surrounding parishes, including Malvern.

Later on, when the Malvern Workhouse had been closed and sold, a Casual Ward Workhouse was built to meet the needs of the wandering poor. This was situated on Malvern Link Common, at the far end of Moorlands Road.

Here, tramps would spend two nights at the House, and for their bed and food, they were required to do work.

One of the tasks was to break granite for road building. The granite would be taken to the Workhouse from North Malvern Quarry and collected when broken. If the tramps refused, they were locked up in cells until they co-operated. They could not stay longer than two nights, and then they were sent on their way.

Until the late 1940's, in summertime, tramps would prefer to sleep in the open, rather than go to the Workhouse. They would curl up in a barn at night and often do a little casual agricultural work during the day."

We see less 'Gentlemen of the Road' nowadays, in rural towns. The present day homeless seem to drift towards big cities.

OLD REMEDIES

Reg Green recalled: "Sometimes my Auntie Harriet and Uncle George came to our home in Guarlford. They had a Herbalist shop in London. We youngsters helped to collect herbs in hessian sacks. We picked betony, scabious, and agrimony. We were paid sixpence a sack. It took us ages to collect a sack full! My Auntie made a green ointment with the herbs. It was a very effective 'cure-all' for all sorts of complaints, including boils and ringworm."

Ellen Hymas remembered: "As a child, I had double pneumonia. My mother put a linseed oil poultice on my chest. I didn't like it! For bee stings, we ran for Mother's blue bag, which she used when washing underclothes to keep them white. For wasp stings? —we put vinegar on them."

"You rubbed camphorated oil on your chest if you had a bad cold", said Mary Tudge.

"I often had bronchitis", lamented Rose Nash. "Brown paper and goose grease was put on my chest, like a poultice. And I had to take Cod Liver oil. So, they gave me lots of Scott's Emulsion in a blue bottle. The label showed a fisherman carrying a large cod over his shoulders. Touch wood, I don't get bronchitis now."

Joy Van Daesdonk recalled several old remedies. "For a bad back, you slapped a sheet of brown paper on it and ironed it. The heat would ease the pain. When my father had bronchitis, an old gentleman arrived at the door with a pot of goose grease.

Some people used to sew themselves up in their winter woollies and not take them off till summer came! For a sore throat, put a stocking you have worn, round your neck. For toothache, a bread poultice was a wonderful thing—put into a cloth and slapped round the chin. It was very comforting."

Alma Longstaff's childhood memories of Saturday nights were not pleasant ones! "Saturday night was the purging night—for all of us seven children. I cried. I used to run a mile! Our parents gave us all Castor Oil. It was vile. But we were allowed a sweet straight afterwards. It was a ritual—and it worked!"

THE END

Gratitudes

• • • • • • • • • • •

(in alphabetical order)

Gordon Acock
Tom Armstrong
Roland Bannister
Winifred Barnes
Brian Beale
Hilda Beale
Ornella Benson
Barbara Bickerstaff
Francis Bird
Geoffrey Boaz
Miss E. Bough
Frank & Mina Bowers
Vivien Bowkley
Dudley Brook
Barbara Brown
David Burley
Frank Burston
Phyllis Castle
Marjorie Chater Hughes
George Chesterton
Geoffrey Chiswell
Nancy Clay
David Cox

Elston Crump
Colin & Helen Cutler
Ivy Dance
Derek Davidson
C. J. Davis
George 'Divvy' Davis
Margaret Davis
Mary Davis
Mary Dixey
Lilian Drinkwater
Nadia Dunning
Peggy Edwards
Patricia Egerton
Bridget Fish
Francis of Malvern
Jim &b Win Foster
Gwen Forster
Betty Gallois-Montbrun
Joan George
Elsie Godsell
Olive Goldsmith
Reg & Joan Green
Gordon Griffith

Wendy Grounds
Elizabeth Guise Berrow
Ethel Hall
Reginald Hall-Robinson
Mrs. Hatfield
Austin Hartwright
Margaret Hands
Stewart Hands
Kathleen Hill
Roy Hodges
Yvonne Hodges
Meriel Hodgetts
Wilf Hoskins
Madge Howard Davies
John Hunt
Ellen Hymas
Elspeth Irwin
Eric Jones
Dorothy Jones
Jean Jones
Lavender Jones
Roger Hall-Jones
Mary Munslow Jones
Elsie Jennings
Marjorie King
Dot Knapper
Albert Layland
Brenda Lawrence
Leslie Lawrence
Louise Lenton
Amy Letchford

Jack Lewis
Lena Lloyd
Maria Lloyd Foulkes
Alma Longstaff
Ken Lynes
Muriel Maby
Agnes McAdam
Frances Milsom
Catherine Moody
Helen Mooney
Audrey Morgan
Dennis Morgan
Peter Morgan
Freda Morris
George Morris
Rose Nash
Dorothy Pembridge
Irene Pitt
Ivy Pitt
Joan Preece
Disney Reynolds
Arthur Russell
May Sadler
George Sayer
Oriana Shaw
Hilda Shinn
Bill Sims
Charles Smith
Doris Smith
Joan Smith
Patricia Soper

Heather Talbot

Gary Taylor

Midge Tompkins

Donald Treherne

Dorothy Treherne

Peter Treherne

Jim Tudge

Mary Tudge

Alan Tyler

Joy Van Daesdonk

Frank Warner

Win Watton

Mary Wells

David Whitehorne

Pam Wootton

I am indebted to the authors of the following books for some appropriate quotations which I have included in my text:

The Silhouette of Malvern—Catherine Moody

Not the Least. The Story of Little Malvern—Ronald Bryer

The Lookers Out of Worcestershire—Mary Munslow Jones

Brays of Malvern Centenary Memoirs booklet of 1995

One Story of Radar—A.P. Rowe

Code Breakers, the Inside Story of Bletchley Park

My Five Cambridge Friends—Yuri Modin

Age Frater (Malvern College Centenary Memoirs) edited by George Sayer

Malvern Girls' College, A Centenary History—Pamela Hurle

I was There—Memories of St. James's School, compiled by Alice Baird

Lawnside, the History of a Malvern School, compiled by Mary Dixey and Duseline Stewart

Journey through the Hills—Boynton

An Organist Remembers—Louis Hamand

I am grateful for the assistance of the following people, firms, or societies:

Malvern Hills Conservators

Coca-Cola and Schweppes of Colwall

Worcester County Archives

Nicholson Organs

Worcestershire County Cricket Club

Worcestershire Beekeepers Association

Worcestershire Golf Club

Elgar Birthplace Museum

I thank Catherine Moody for the loan of the drawing of Troyte Griffith and the painting of George Bernard Shaw, both created by her father, Victor Hume Moody.

I thank and acknowledge the following people for the use of photographs:

Christine Bannister

Roland Bannister

Hilda Beale

Francis Bird

Minna Bowers

Arthur Brown

David Burley

Marjorie Chater Hughes

Madge Howard Davies

George 'Divvy' Davis

Margaret Davis

Gwen Forster

Meriel Hodgetts
Wilf Hoskins
Alma Longstaff
Dennis Morgan
Peter Morgan
Arthur Russell
Heather Talbot
Midge Tompkins
Jim Tudge

Mary Tudge
Malvern College
Malvern Girls' College
Cridlan and Walker
Brays of Malvern
Malvern Gazette &
  Ledbury Reporter
Norman May's Studio
  Worcester

Thank you for reading
This Was OUR Malvern ~ Worcestershire
& Malvern History Series Book 2

● ●

You might also enjoy *From Cottage to Palace ~*
Worcestershire & Malvern History Series Book 1
https://www.amazon.com/dp/B09WB2LQHM
and the audiobook on Audible:
https://www.audible.com/pd/From-Cottage-
to-Palace-Audiobook/B0B3PQTSGZ
and
Upton-Upon-Severn Recollections ~
Worcestershire & Malvern History Series Book 3
https://www.amazon.com/gp/product/B0B1QX1BZ8

For more information about the Worcestershire
& Malvern History Series by Margaret Bramford,
or to sign up for our FREE richardlynttonbooks
(fiction and nonfiction) newsletter, VISIT
this richardlynttonbooks website link:

https://richardlynttonbooks.com/contact/

If you enjoyed the book, we would very much
appreciate it if you could leave a review on the
platform you used. Thank you so much!